Other Books by Wallace Fowlie

Journal of Rehearsals: A Memoir
Aubade: A Teacher's Notebook
Sites: A Third Memoir
Letters of Henry Miller and Wallace Fowlie
Characters from Proust: Poems
A Reading of Dante's Inferno
A Reading of Proust
Mallarmé
Rimbaud: A Critical Study
André Gide: His Life and Art
Paul Claudel
Stendhal
The French Critic
Climate of Violence
Dionysus in Paris
Age of Surrealism
The Clown's Grail (Love in Literature)
Clowns and Angels

TRANSLATIONS

Complete Works of Rimbaud
Two Dramas by Claudel
A Poet before the Cross by Claudel
Seamarks by Saint-John Perse
Don Juan by Molière
Classical French Drama (Five Plays)
Mid-Century French Poems
Sixty Poems of Scève

Collection of W.F.

Wallace Fowlie

MEMORY

A Fourth Memoir

for Jan— in memory of th summer of 1994 love. Wallie

Duke University Press
Durham and London 1990

Portions of the following chapters, usually rewritten, were
originally published as separate articles in the following
magazines: "Memory": *The Sewanee Review*, Vol. 97,
No. 2, April–June 1989. "Remembering Jacques
Maritain": *The American Scholar*, Volume 56, No. 3,
Summer 1987. "Remembering Renan": *The American
Scholar*, Volume 58, No. 2, Spring 1989. "Pasolini's
Teorema": *Evergreen Review*. Volume 14, No. 74, January
1970. "*Poetry Magazine* Is 75 Years Old": *Poetry*, October–
November 1987 (75th Anniversary Issue). "Remembering
Léonie Adams": *The New Criterion*, Volume 7, No. 2,
October 1988.

Library of Congress Cataloging-in-Publication Data
Fowlie, Wallace, 1908–
Memory : a fourth memoir / Wallace Fowlie.
p.   cm.
Includes index.
ISBN 0-8223-1003-1
ISBN 0-8223-1045-7 (pbk.)
1. Fowlie, Wallace, 1908–.   2. French teachers—United States—
Biography.   3. Critics—United States—Biography.   I. Title.
PQ67.F65A3   1990
840.9—dc20
[B]   89-35872

to Porfirio Roggi

Contents

PART I

CHAPTER 1

Memory

We call it now "stream of consciousness," but through the centuries memory, for want of a better term, has been referred to as flowing water. During these past ten years I have descended into that stream more often than I have stayed on its banks, on the solid ground of day-by-day life. Currents of the past are indeed deep, and at times I have struggled hard to raise my ghosts, watery figures mist-covered, in order to join them and walk again with them.

Self-writing, with which I am now unashamedly allied, is, in a fundamental sense, mimesis. It has its grandeur, and its misery too. But it has the music of human life. I can still hear the waves breaking on South Beach in Popham, which I heard when I was nine years old, as clearly as I hear this morning, at the age of seventy-nine, the cars rushing along Chapel Hill Boulevard on their way to Chapel Hill or Durham.

The eternal moment: that is the sole subject of autobiography. I am who I was. Life is a narrative, and self-writing is narrative discourse, whether I am recalling a specific episode, or the words of a friend, or thoughts that rise up again and again in my consciousness. When I say to myself, "observe each day as it comes in, and celebrate it as if it is an *aubade*," I am really saying, "observe age as it comes in, and make it serviceable."

I have lived through an age of innocence, and I have lived through an age of adversity. It is time now for me to begin to know an age of

reconciliation. These are words of a narrative. They form the plot
of the oldest type of myth—the related parts of a sequence: innocence (or what I might call "childhood"), adversity (which might
be the trials and wanderings of an initiation), and finally a reconciliation of the memories of childhood and the scars of initiation,
of the *rites de passage*. The final revelation may be a glimmer in the
dark or a blinding flash.

I pursue a lonely conception of this book and often say to myself
as I resume daily work on it: where is its grand design? I persevere
because I am the sole custodian of the figures of my life. Those invisible presences play their part as I rehearse the repetitive patterns
of living. There was, of course, at the beginning an original text, a
first occurrence. But then, each year, each decade, the original text
is reworked. For Dante Alighieri it became one of his one hundred
cantos, written perhaps in Verona, in his exile from Florence. For
Ezra Pound it became one of his *Pisan Cantos,* also written in exile,
possibly in Rapallo.

Such master craftsmen as they were are examples for minor
writers who live in far less dramatic exiles. From such writers,
and from others—Pascal, St. Augustine, Thomas Merton—I have
learned that what I have been seeking I have already found. From
the writing of these pages I know that I am going to where I am.
Circularity in time and space is the mode of my existence as I recall
words and sites, figures and sounds, desolation and jubilation.

Places, real places where I once lived, are more real than the town
in which I now live. And they haunt me and draw me back through
intervening spaces: a street in Boston, a hotel in Nice, a eucalyp-
tus tree in Taormina, a movie house in New Haven, New York's
Central Park, Gold Hill, Colorado. Paris is my pillar of cloud and
fire. I have crouched on Golgotha and watched through the night
the figure praying there and suffering.

For many years I have lived so close to Dante that I now behold
life in images of journeying, and especially in images of *descent*. And
yet I am related to no hero, to no protagonist comparable to Dante.
Wherever I am, it is a place of no thoroughfare. I have lived in places
of no movement—in the Flora Hotel, for example, in Rome. And
I have lived in places where all was movement—in the Pensione

Beacci in Florence. If I had the strength of no purpose, I would drop all props and wander forth. Then I would feel more related to a hero and more able to resist this need to write of the self.

In retrospect I can remember clearly the unique power of Paris. It obliterated for me all personal affairs, all personal attachments. I had read *Le Père Goriot* and *Le spleen de Paris*, and thus in the streets of Paris I dreamed not of myself but of Balzac's Eugène de Rastignac and *Le vieux saltimbanque* of Baudelaire. There I learned to think of books as artifacts, as objects not related to me but to truth, and when I came upon the sentence (I believe it is Flaubert's), *Tout ce qu'on invente est vrai* (Everything invented is true), I knew I had discovered a major key to the art of reading and the art of teaching. The old writers of France—Villon and Ronsard, Rousseau and Nerval—were *revenants* for me whom I welcomed in my *promenades,* whom I accosted at times and on whose marginal imaginative world I poached.

What indulgence for me: those spontaneous offerings of memory! From my earliest visits to France, when I lived in Montparnasse and ate at Mme Yvet's *pension* table, I knew that those pages of memory, a *pensée* of Pascal, a *dizain* of Scève, were more real than the daily chatter I heard and contributed to. The French, more than the people of other nations, have a deep respect for books, for the great books of their past. They know that books are built like pyramids—for endurance and for the protection of life in words that will never vanish. When I first read Proust, I followed particularly the drama of human relationships. On subsequent rereadings I began following the way in which he built his novel, quite similar, I imagine, to the way in which the Egyptians built their pyramids.

My inner life has experienced too little guilt and too little despair. Thus my life has been too drab, too thin. This urge to write about it is most certainly an effort to alter its drabness by understanding it better, by allowing memory to work its miracle. I experience almost simultaneously two kinds of excitement: the pull to chronicle and the pull to compose a work of art.

Autobiography is fiction of a special breed. One picture is always clear in my mind when I hear the word: a young man from his province en route to the city (and the city is usually Paris). Flaubert,

Balzac, Stendhal, of course, but also James Joyce, Rimbaud, Hart Crane, St. Augustine, Thomas Merton. The pattern is the same, but the adventures and the goals differ.

The personal growth in each of these famous men is unique, and that is what autobiography means, that is the meaning of a *Bildungsroman*. In this comparison I am making with these great names and accomplishments, my own personal growth, if I can call it that, is linguistic. I study words in order to become more human. Words at first not understood, but spoken over and over until I have learned them by heart. Separate isolated words first, in this process of turning myself into a human being, and then whole poems (*Mémoire* of Rimbaud, or "Vergine Madre," canto 33, *Il Paradiso*); then whole scenes from Molière (*Les Femmes Savantes*) and Racine (*Phèdre*).

Some of this language studied is soon reduced to shibboleths, and I discard them. In the same way I learn and then discard new words used today for sexual and emotional development. The Bible words, "spikenard, myrrh, and frankincense," reworked in *A Portrait of the Artist as a Young Man*, as Stephen Dedalus listens to them, have all the qualities of poetry and magic which have lived in my memory since early childhood. Beautiful words for a child, but meaningless. I had to add years to my life before I began to understand them.

In the same chapter Joyce uses the phrase *non serviam* (I will not serve). Stephen is listening to a sermon on Lucifer's pride. The entire course of mythology and history seemed to be in those two Latin words: Dedalus and Icarus, Lucifer, and Stephen in the twentieth century. Whenever now I see or use "rebel" and "rebellion," *non serviam* comes to my mind. From these two words I feel not only a poetic impact, associated with Dedalus, Icarus, Lucifer, Stephen, but a visceral one as well. *Non serviam* is linked to the most persistent autobiographical pattern. In those words I hear defiance, and then I see a picture: a hawklike boy flying sunward. And then I turn to the words of a text (used, I suppose, in the sermon listened to by Stephen): "For God spared not the angels that sinned, but cast them down to hell" (2 Peter 2:4).

I cannot separate words from memory. One is linked to the other. It is a marriage in a way, as mysterious as the fusion I often catch myself making of sensuality and sanctity: another pair of words, comparable to *non serviam,* in the sense of providing the design and the plot of a life story. Each of Joyce's three books—*A Portrait, Ulysses, Finnegans Wake*—and each of the seven parts of Proust's *A la recherche* is an ever-deepening plunge into autobiography, where the father searches for his son and where the son searches for his father. The mystery of paternity is in Stephen-Bloom, in Marcel-Swann, in Ham-Noah, in the words of Jesus to his Father ("let this cup pass from my hands").

The beginning of life is also its ending. Since life is fluidity, its dramatic finality is not played out here on this earth. A seemingly trivial small act determines our life, and that is why I wish to remember, in this fourth attempt at remembering, such an act, with such an encounter in my own life. But not before I rehearse once more the sense of a vocation which grew in me mysteriously in Paris and in Cambridge, Massachusetts. That vocation depended on words, foreign words derived from a dead language. It depended also on a need to journey, to impose upon myself, more than thirty times, a self-exile. I had to find fresh words, and learn how to use them, if I wanted to survive.

That journeying forth, at first from Cambridge to Paris and in later years from North Carolina to Paris and to Florence, always followed the pattern of a search for words, and in a more mystical, more concealed sense a search for a son-father relationship. I gradually grew conscious of the degree to which the narrative patterns of the Bible had formed me, and the obedience I was demonstrating in searching for that pattern. Often I felt lost in the cycle of generations I read in Genesis: the role of Abraham and God's command to multiply so that the race would equal the stars in the heavens; the rivalry of Cain and Abel; the story of young Joseph and the older sons. I was an only son, and I envied the role of a favored son, a divine son.

The story of Moses and God's burning bush was like a root planted in me, an identification I made with young and old Moses. The sun in the heavens never failed to illuminate and restore me, but I sought too to feel connected with the sources under the earth, with the roots, with the life of trees. Was this demonic knowledge that I sought in roots, as I sought divine knowledge in the sun?

Only in the task of narrative will I find myself. With my real father I had very little conversation, and that is why I turned—unconsciously—to fathers in the Bible, in mythology, and in novels. I heeded the words of young Joseph's father in the Old Testament, and I meditated on the figure of Joseph, father of Our Lord in the New Testament. In my late adolescence fictional fathers held me strongly and fostered all my fantasies: le marquis de la Môle receiving Julien Sorel so graciously in his Paris residence. And then especially Charles Swann in Proust's novel showing young Marcel pictures of Renaissance art, and later in the book the sadness of Marcel when he saw in an imposing salon scene the unmistakable signs of death on the face of the older Swann when he reached the age of prophet.

In those years I yearned for a state of bondage so that I might follow the pattern of growth, marriage, fatherhood, and death. In exile from paternal conversation and from maternal embrace, I sought new forms of vitality in being more urgent, more insistent, by wishing to be a father. When I lost my innocence with a girl —she and I were both sixteen—I felt half-afraid and childish after the immensity of passion. We were Adam and Eve who had lost our innocence in Paradise and knew we would be driven out of Paradise.

It was the dawn of humanity for me, and for a short period thereafter, on every starry night, I returned to the scene of biblical creation. There I felt as nothing. There I knew that self-creation in words was the one way for survival. I read from Acts, chapter nine, what the Lord had said to Paul: "Arise, and go into the city, and it shall be told thee what thou must do." When I put pen to paper in those days of confusion, I myself was not writing; I was writing myself. I was following a tradition, by imitating all those who had written before me. Even those details that seemed unique when I wrote them adhered to an archetypal pattern.

I was vaguely unhappy at that time, without knowing why. I lived in constant expectation of being accused, without knowing of what. Some years later in a gathering of friends in Boston, which included two navy psychiatrists, we were talking in a random way of great ideas—Nietzsche, Freud, socialism, psychoanalysis —when I began to realize that everyone in the room, except myself, had undergone psychoanalysis. I announced to them all that I felt outside the group, ostracized from the fraternity. They laughed then, and one of them said—he was the friend who knew me best —"You have as many neuroses as the rest of us do, but no doctor would take you on, if you asked to be psychoanalyzed, simply because you have no guilt, you are not suffering, you have adjusted to your neuroses. Teaching is your perpetual therapy. And writing is your substitute therapy during the few hours when you are not teaching."

I should have said to my doctor friend at that moment—but my wits were floundering and I kept silence—"Rereading my favorite biblical stories gives me some degree of psychological health: all those stories between the first Incarnation, Adam's, and the second, Christ's."

In these later years the writing of my past has replaced a doctor's therapy. My book is a mirror, the legitimate place for both good and evil, the reconciler of opposites.

The usual cycle in a man's life of exile and return to the home base, is, in my case, the cycle of exile and a further exile in a new place. There has been no return home. Boston-Cambridge to Connecticut (Taft School and Yale), to Chicago, to Vermont (Bennington), to Colorado (Boulder), to North Carolina (Durham). And now at Duke, where I still teach long after I should legitimately have retired, I contemplate the next move, one not too far from this place of favorite courses, and medicine, and the thwarted hope of building a chapel on Campus Drive, which I planned to call "Chapel of the Angels" to offset the "Blue Devils."

In this act of writing autobiography I feel no boundaries in the past or future. To prepare for such an act, sleep has become a mode of existence. There, in the ever-moving realms of sleep, fables are what count and not history. Myths would be a stronger word. They reveal aspects of truth concerning human destiny. In early childhood I had knowledge of immortality, and later in my life, in the story of a boy I intend to relate in this book, my knowledge of immortality was renewed.

A child perceives many things without knowing the words with which to name them. A grown man perceives far less: he remains within the closed realm of ignorance, of desire, and of ambition. When I first talked with the child of my narrative, I knew that prior to his advent I had been living among an awkward human race whose innocence had been lost, where power had diminished. As I watched the child, the fear grew in me that the world would beat him down. I had never felt such pathos before. The pathos was in me, not in him. Fatherless, he had fallen into my life.

My essays and books of literary criticism are today my quarries. Thanks to them, this new text I am writing can be stabilized. Let me be self-writer now and not critic.

Whatever this chronicle is, whatever it becomes, I know it is rooted in the reading of literature, and in the exercises I have written about French writers and Dante. There has been little or no influence from other autobiographers. Almost nothing from Rousseau and Yeats. Some, it is true, from Thoreau, and some from Henry Adams. And that is because I already knew their woods and cities. I remembered the fields and ponds of New England. I remembered Boston and Paris, the Virgin of Notre Dame, Louisburg Square, the Church of the Advent.

I write, then, not from private fantasy, but rather from a cultural endowment, attracted by rhythms of prose and a biblical Paradise. As I try to relate my traditions, I am aware of the fragmentariness of images.

But they are the images I have taken over for myself. I learned to live with them in my own lonely tower—perhaps not a tower, but a cavern hidden from sight. Reflections (both images and thoughts) became my psychic research—in which the Irish part of my makeup needed no Madame Blavatsky.

The personalities of my teachers in early adolescence, and, later, the personalities of my Harvard professors, form a meandering succession that I have mythologized, who have become me in some unique metamorphosis. I hear them in my voice and see them in gestures I make in my classroom.

Two impulses to write more are the genesis of this fourth attempt to explain my life to myself. The first is my early study in Paris and my meeting with Jacques Maritain and Noémi Renan. I needed to record somehow, somewhere details of those encounters I had not heretofore recorded. The second—a far different experience—was the repeated vision I had of a boy appearing under a catalpa tree and staring at my house.

The first was the work of learning and study; the other was a contact with a living being, with life presenting itself to me as tragedy. Today, with some perspective, I realize that not until those two moments had passed did I begin to live with a fuller awareness of destiny. It was first my reaching out to a cultural ideal, and then it was a life touching my life. Initially, an image grew in my mind —an idealized picture—and then the epiphany itself, the full and yet fragile manifestation.

A saintly man of wisdom and a boy pushed me through the gate of mythologies into the experience behind all stories. I moved beyond Dante and Villon, beyond a comedy and a tragedy.

Visions they are now—and hence these pages—and my varied commentaries about them still leave me unknowing about their meaning. Yet they still absorb me and force me to speculate. I reached, if I can believe my own uncertain understanding, an epiphanic moment. So strong was it that I still question what is to follow, what has followed, in my uncertain destiny.

Do I go against nature in this constant attempt to fill my life with writing about life? I have, without ever consciously attempting to cultivate it, a typological habit of mind. I have been Adam, whose handsome sons were dead. I have been David, exploiting the death of Uriah. And from each of such figures I claim a personal rebirth, a survival in history. Figures of quest they are, by means of which many paths are mapped.

This fictional guise that I am calling autobiography is made up of conventions and mythologies that frame half-truths. A meeting of minds took place—not in reading Rimbaud, but in trying to explain him in a classroom. The presence of others around me, of young lives—innocent despite all their worldliness and sophistication—has forced me into moments of self-identification. I would never have written about Rimbaud if I had not taught him. I would never have written a memoir-book if I had not half-memorized *Une saison en enfer*.

The artful flashes that fill *Une saison* portray man rather than one man. The narrator in that work is also the protagonist—as Proust was once in *A la recherche* so gloriously, so ruthlessly. With such models which I observed by teaching them, I have been forced to exhibit myself twice over: an outworn self, and a new self which these words create. Self-scrutiny leads me to beings outside myself. How futile to hope for any total autobiographical image!

As an older narrator I learn now to manipulate pseudoauto-biographical forms. Have I reread too often? Have I thought too steadfastly of the past? Have sentences and rhythms of Rimbaud (*L'automne déjà!*) persisted too long in my memory? There is a covert religion at work in Rimbaud's text. One day in the future it will lie exposed for all to see. All men are one. Every text, even *Une saison*, will be demystified.

Without the support of literature, no one can have an image of humanity, no one can have a theory of life. Books of science lead into literature, but they lack the splendor, the portentous truths of *Four Quartets*, of *Ulysses*, of *Lear*. It is, after all, racial memory that counts, the transmission of experience from generation to generation: Boethius to Dante to Chaucer to Machiavelli. Only after such a genealogy will a man begin to comprehend such a figure as *Fortuna*.

We are continuous from generation to generation. The embryo that turned into the child I once was, and which is now an old man, will not have reached the end at my death. Concerned as we are with our bodily changes, we early forget the transmigration of our soul that is also taking place when we breathe and when we will no longer breathe.

I rarely watch sunsets, but each morning for the past thirty years I have watched the sunrise, even when a gray mist covers it and there is no visible sun. I have seen it rise over Lake Como and over Mount Etna, over housetops in Paris, and over the distant Medi-terranean from my hotel room in Saint-Paul-de-Vence. At such unusual mornings as those in my life, I joined the coming of dawn in my eyes to the inner light of my spirit as it strove to pierce the darkened mystery of words on the page of a notebook.

Light veils of clouds have allowed me to converse more frankly with Dante and Montaigne, with Saint John in Patmos, and Jules Laforgue in his Pierrot complaints. Such men have been my fellow travelers. And they often kept me outside the major movements of my plot. Now that I look back more often than I look forward, I journey back on the road of ancestry, to emperors and pontifices, to gallows victims and court jesters. I must be after some theory of recovery I am unable to resurrect. A seminal source in the sun, perhaps. A myth fostered in my childhood as I walked on paths around Walden Pond. I have moved from pagan learning to letters of Paul.

Truth is to be found in autobiographical fable. I try to hear voices that echo in the pages of this narrative, and often recognize them to be echoes of my fledgling selves. I remain principally an early naive *persona*.

Much of my life, and of the lives before mine, is invisible in a Lethean darkness. The commanding spirit of my grandmother, Mary Ann Adams, is a *dea ex machina*. If I could reach her more lucidly, more directly, many confusions would clear. She is there in my memory, as she was in life when as a child I served her in minor ways. Powerful yet immobile in her large parlor chair, she persisted as a standard of truth and clarity. She had worked hard, first in Ireland (Belfast), and then in America (Boston) during the sixty years before my birth. During the first ten years of my life she observed the toils of all the members of her family: her husband, her four daughters, and their offspring. All the male figures, within a radius of miles, were rendered impotent in her presence. She remained within the house always. No need to sit outside under the sun. She was the sun, the center.

There was no need then, in the last years of her life, to go to the Harvard Congregational Church at Coolidge Corner, Brookline. Its members came to her, bearing with them a portable organ, and there, in her own parlor, a man and two ladies each week would sing hymns that I had helped her choose. She was proud of this attention, but with me when we selected the next week's hymns, she would parody the gestures and the speech of that strange trio that arrived each Wednesday afternoon before her door, in a slow-moving electric automobile.

Grandmother Adams reduced the sacrosanct intentions of those church visitors to comic techniques. I laughed because she demanded that, but I was inwardly puzzled and saddened by her attitude. I argued to myself: she is alive, but she is also in the midst of death. She seemed so old! And yet she was defeating death at all points. Because of my grandmother, I have all my life disliked the casual kind of humor that mocks the traits of a serious human being.

I attended very few of my grandmother's hymn concerts. One I remember better than the others, when the first hymn to be sung was "In the Cross of Christ I Glory." The high notes were too high for the soprano lady, and the gentleman organist had to stop, transpose the music into a lower key, and begin the singing again. I knew my grandmother would comment on that event throughout the following week, and she did. Not to others in the family, but only to me, her helper in her weekly diversion.

If the hymns were fairly simple, the organist would blow the note A on his tuning pipe, and the two ladies would sing without accompaniment. This always seemed too bare, too embarrassing to my grandmother and me. We preferred to have the voices somewhat covered up by the puffing and swelling of the organ notes.

Before I knew the word "typology," I saw myself in biblical characters. Through them my life had a divine underwriting. Such transformations were easy for me. There had been no rural innocence characterizing my early years. The Bible had been a great teacher of misdemeanors and sins. After every reading of the flood, I was reunited with friends and with the stalwart figure of Noah. My early school compositions were not about myself, but about Ham and Joseph and Samson whom I disguised in my use of the first person pronoun. Like an innocent thief, I enhanced my personal identity.

Biblical scenes of innocence and exile characterized my barely protected state of childhood. As they unfolded in my mind, I instinctively turned away from all tawdry realism and all Words-worthian pastoral. I realize now, at a much later time, that the incompleteness of autobiography may have the effect of falsity. Was I, and am I still, bound to reticence for the piety I owe others—family and friends? Is this a form of self-ignorance? Self-betrayal? I think not. I have never wanted to be a weepy self-pleader.

The image of life as a river flowing along and being fed by tribu-tary streams, and whose entrance into the sea is death, is an arche-type long in the race of man. The growth of the river accumulating riches is the preparation for annihilation, for expansion and then dissolution. It fits perfectly the nature of tragedy, which is life-death. As a child, I watched the mouth of the Kennebec River at the sea, and now I am writing that experience.

I am waiting now for a climactic flood that will fulfill the action lived heretofore as an obscure drama. The Charles River of my childhood, and the Seine and the Arno I watched in later years, are less significant to me than the river of *Le Bateau Ivre*. In that river, and in the river of another of Rimbaud's poems, *Mémoire*, I felt the beatings of the world's mighty heart. They were the outlet toward something noble and beautiful.

CHAPTER 2

Remembering Jacques Maritain:
Paris—Meudon—New York—New Haven

Only twice in my very long career as a teacher of French have I given a public lecture on Jacques Maritain. Forty years ago, soon after the beginning of my career, I spoke to the Renascence Society in Manhattan, and in December 1985 I spoke from personal notes on my relationship with Jacques to members of the Maritain Association in Atlanta. In that audience there were several former students and friends. The name of Jacques Maritain had counted in our friendship, and I reminded them that my friendship with Jacques had preceded by many years my friendship with them. Longevity was the explanation of that state of affairs. My first meeeting with Jacques Maritain was more than half a century earlier, at the very beginning of my career. I was trying to tell them that I held a record: memories that go back farther in time than their memories, memories of Jacques that are inextricably tied in with the names of poets—the Symbolist poets of France, and Dante and Eliot, precisely those poets I have been trying to teach to American students over the past fifty years.

The history of that record I hold, which put me in a spotlight I enjoyed at that Atlanta meeting, is made up of phases. As I mentioned them in an effort of recollection, my listeners might have believed them to be chance encounters, chance happenings, juxtapositions of the same names that return persistently. But I do not really believe in chance. It does not explain the pattern, the design of my life, which I am still trying to see and understand.

The name of Jacques Maritain was never mentioned in any of the college courses I took as an undergraduate. Two of my professors might have referred to him (André Morize and Irving Babbitt), but they never did. However, in 1932–33, when I was a graduate student at Harvard and an instructor in French there, I heard Jacques's name first mentioned in a classroom by T. S. Eliot. It was the year of Eliot's Charles Eliot Norton lectures. His contract called for him to give, in addition to the six public lectures, a course limited to fifteen students on English literature between 1890 and 1930. I had the privilege of taking that course. The reference Eliot made to Maritain was related to a somewhat critical attitude toward nineteenth-century French literature and especially romanticism.

During my senior year at Harvard, 1929–30, I had taken a famous course by Irving Babbitt, called "Rousseau and Romanticism," in which Babbitt, with whom Eliot had studied and about whom he had written an important essay, had been much more vehemently hostile than Eliot to the entire nineteenth century in France, to romanticism at the beginning of the century, and to the movement at the end of the century which, with scorn in his voice, he called "decadence," and which, like romanticism, he traced back to Jean-Jacques Rousseau.

In 1932 Eliot, more gentle, more soft-toned, than Babbitt, spoke in that class I attended of the development of positivism in France in the nineteenth century. It was then that he spoke of Jacques Maritain, of neo-Thomism, and of its efforts to counteract positivism.

In addition to his public lectures and his class of fifteen students, Eliot received for tea every Wednesday afternoon in his rooms in Eliot House the fifteen members of his class. At those teas which we never missed, several of the students made bold to ask about the meaning of lines in Eliot's poems, especially lines from *Ash-Wednesday* which had just been published in 1930. Mr. Eliot never answered those questions on the meaning of specific lines.

On one of those semisocial occasions, I brought up the name of Maritain, which was new to me, and asked Eliot what book of his I should read. His answer came quickly: "Rather than reading Maritain's first book, on Bergson, I recommend *Art et scolastique*." The following morning I discovered it was not yet in Widener Library, and so I ordered a copy for myself from Paris.

At another Wednesday tea, somewhat in my role of French major (the other students were all English majors), I asked Eliot what French authors of the nineteenth century we could read without being "contaminated." That was one of Babbitt's favorite words, and I felt sure Eliot would recognize it. He did, and smiled as he answered, "I know where you got that word." What he said then was an important command for me: "Read Mallarmé, and those poets who come after Mallarmé."

When my copy of *Art et scolastique* reached me (it was the second edition of 1927), there I found Mallarmé's name and those poets who followed Mallarmé. I must have taken Eliot's advice to heart because today, a half century later, I am still working on Mallarmé's *Prose pour des Esseintes*, and Maritain's *Art et scolastique*.

By that time in my college career, as might be guessed, there was a cluster of names causing some bewilderment in the mind of a French major who was already teaching and wondering what subject he might be given for his doctoral thesis. The names were Babbitt and Rousseau, Eliot and Mallarmé, and finally the new name of Jacques Maritain.

Professor Babbitt had a favorite phrase he used in denouncing the French nineteenth century, a phrase that Eliot must have heard. Babbitt lectured in English, but this phrase he always gave in French and ascribed to a large variety of critics. We students had decided that Babbitt had made it up himself, and named as its author those critics he deemed sufficiently intelligent to have coined the phrase. It was: *ce stupide dix-neuvième siècle*. Babbitt was a powerful teacher. He impressed upon all of us the danger, the moral danger, of reading nineteenth-century French literature.

But there was now for me one way of salvaging the century in its poets at the end, poets Babbitt probably had not studied. That way had been pointed out to me by Eliot, and the poets were there, commented on by Maritain in *Art et scolastique*: Baudelaire, Mallarmé, Rimbaud, and two from our own century: Max Jacob and Jean Cocteau.

Even in *Art et scolastique* I saw Maritain not only as philosopher-aesthetician but as a contemplative. During my senior year and the Eliot year at Harvard, I attended services regularly at the Anglican chapel of the Cowley Fathers in Cambridge on the Charles River. During 1932 and 1933 I was assigned to be server at mass every Tuesday—an early mass, celebrated at that time in a very small chapel. Eliot was a daily communicant. I saw him therefore every Tuesday morning. He was often the only one present, with the priest and myself.

One of those Tuesday mornings was especially memorable, more than the Monday, Wednesday, Friday mornings in the classroom in Sever. As always at that mass Eliot came up to the altar step to receive communion. After receiving, he returned to his seat (he was the only person in the small nave of the chapel) and the priest and I turned back to the altar. We heard then a heavy thud, and turned around somewhat startled to see Mr. Eliot flat on his stomach, his arms outstretched. I felt certain he was praying, but the priest was worried (this was not usual behavior in an Anglican chapel) and he said to me, "What shall we do?" In the spirit of a real organizer, I said, "Let's finish up here first." We did turn back and the priest finished his mass.

When we turned around again, Eliot was still stretched out, his face pressed against the floor. Then the Cowley father took over by saying, "He may be ill, help him up." I put my arm under Eliot's shoulder, and he came up easily with me. There was no trouble in seating him. Never, in subsequent Wednesday teas, did he refer to that episode, which I believe to have been a religious experience.

Jacques Maritain possessed an extraordinary power to change the lives of his friends, of uniting them with him and with one another, of opening them up to his ideas, or rather to the ideas he served. The second phase of this narrative is my actual meeting with Jacques and the reason for that meeting.

The summer following Eliot's year at Harvard I spent in Paris reading works largely from what is sometimes called "the Catholic Renaissance in French literature," works often inspired by *Art et scolastique*: Péguy, Bloy, Claudel, and others. I had been assigned a topic, quite arbitrarily (which was the custom then) for my dissertation. My thesis director, André Morize, had told me to write on the poetry of Sainte-Beuve. At that time we were supposed to find a topic that had not been written about. When I read Sainte-Beuve's poetry, I realized clearly why it had not been written about. I had been reading Baudelaire and Mallarmé, and feeling exalted by such poetry. By the end of that summer I was depressed with thoughts of returning to Sainte-Beuve in Cambridge.

Then a totally unexpected meeting took place which changed my life. Apparently by chance, I wandered one day at the end of summer—it was the day before I was to take the boat home—into an attractive new bookstore on the rue Denfert-Rochereau. I had noticed in the window display a new edition of Pascal's *Pensées*, edited by Henri Massis, one of the Catholic critics I had been reading that summer. A striking woman, who turned out to be the owner of the shop, waited on me, showed me the Pascal volume, and spoke so knowingly about Pascal and Henri Massis that I began asking her about other books of that nature. By then she had become aware of my interest in religious writings and asked, "Have you read Jacques Maritain?"

I told her I had read only *Antimoderne* and *Art et scolastique*. Then came the second key question, "Do you know the books of my brother?" I had to say, "Madame, I do not know who you are. I came in here by chance. Who is your brother?"

"My brother is Ernest Psichari. I am Henriette Psichari."

At that very moment in my *pension* room in Paris there was a copy of Psichari's *Voyage du centurion*, which I had bought but not yet read. Vaguely I remembered that Psichari had some family relationship with Ernest Renan whom I had studied in a course on *ce stupide dix-neuvième siècle*. I asked Mme Psichari about the relationship and she said, "Yes, I am the granddaughter of Renan." I recalled then a reference to Renan in *Art et scolastique*.

She continued by saying, "I questioned you first about Maritain because he was my brother's closest friend." At that time I was unaware of that relationship.

Before I left the bookstore I ordered the other three books by Psichari and asked permission to write to Henriette Psichari about them once I had returned to Cambridge. Already in my mind that morning in Paris I was plotting an escape from Sainte-Beuve, and a change of thesis subject.

I knew, however, that this would cause a minor drama in Cambridge and began dreading my first meeting that fall with Professor Morize. When I found myself in his office in Widener Library, I went immediately to the problem: "Is it possible for me to change the subject of my dissertation?"

"No," he said. "It's an ideal subject for you. You are interested in poetry. Sainte-Beuve's poetry has not been written about." As a conclusive argument, to make me squirm all the more, he added, "I have been saving this topic for you."

Then came a pause, after the explosion. "What other subject do you have in mind?"

My answer was a test for Morize. I said simply, "Ernest Psichari." After a few seconds of silence, he said (and passed the test), "You mean the grandson of Renan?"

"Yes."

"Not possible! It's much too recent a subject for Harvard. The department would never allow it."

Another pause, and then a second objection, stronger than the first. "You'd have to get the family's permission. Psichari died at the beginning of the war." (Morize had been a captain in the French army.)

I tried then not to appear too cocky and said, "I believe I can have that permission."

"What makes you say that?"

Thereupon I told my professor the little story about the bookstore on the rue Denfert-Rochereau. Since my professor was a Frenchman, I emphasized the beauty of Mme Psichari and her erudition.

A still longer pause; then, with his final words, he dismissed me: "Write for that permission, and then we will talk."

I received permission from both Psichari's sister and his mother.

In each of the two following winters I spent a month in the home of Mme Noémi Renan, daughter of Renan and mother of Psichari. (The ladies in that family were divorced and had taken back their maiden name.) Thus I was able to secure the documentation I needed and enjoy the conversation each lunch and dinner of a remarkable lady, in the very house where Ernest Psichari had lived: 16, rue Chaptal.

On my arrival the first winter the sister and the mother drew up a list of names of people who had known Psichari and who might be willing to talk with me. At the top of the list, as the friend who knew Psichari the best, was the name of Jacques Maritain.

I must say that this was a very generous suggestion because the sister and the mother were not at all in accord with Maritain. Noémi Renan was very close to the thought and convictions and even to the style of speech of her famous father. Henriette Psichari often spoke strongly against Maritain's philosophy and political convictions. Both were convinced that Maritain was responsible for Psichari's conversion, which they deplored. However, they both urged me to see him by claiming he was the principal key to my research.

I wrote therefore to the Meudon address they gave me: 10, avenue du Parc. The answer was an appointment for the following week.

In order to prepare for that meeting—in order to see Maritain and hear him before I met him—I attended one of his lectures in his course at the Institut Catholique—a small class, about twelve students, with whom I sat for several minutes before Maritain came in. A quiet, swift entrance, a brief prayer as we all stood, and then the lesson began, or rather continued from the previous meeting. It was a course based on his recently published book, *Les degrés du savoir*, obviously a difficult book, one that needed the explanations that the author was giving. (Much later Henry Bars was to call *Les degrés du savoir* Maritain's most important philosophical book.)

The lesson at the Institut Catholique was hard, but by listening to the philosopher-teacher discuss and explain isolated sentences from his own text, I was to be helped in my first encounter with Jacques the following week in Meudon. The walk from the station to 10, avenue du Parc was auspiciously sun-flooded. The house rested on the flank of a small hill overlooking Paris. The city from which I had come was spread out there below, distantly veiled by smoke and haze.

I was shown into a long, sparsely furnished room. The few

chairs and a table, and especially the few pictures on the wall, converted the room's natural austerity into subtle refinement. The house seemed totally silent as soon as the maid had closed the door behind her. I walked to the end of the room to look at a very poignant sketch of a face I recognized as Baudelaire's.

After a few minutes, M. Maritain came in, closed the door behind him, and moved rapidly across the room to greet me and sit down in a chair nearest to mine. I had seen faces resembling his in paintings of Modigliani. The broad line of his brow and the lower part of his face tapering to a fine point emphasized the importance and almost the autonomy of his head. The shock of graying hair falling across his forehead, seeming to incline his face to one side, added a youthful expression to a face that belonged to no particular age.

His presence led me into myself. The questions I had prepared in my mind, and on paper too, began to appear irrelevant, or to answer themselves. In their place, problems more exciting and central and imperative formed without my knowing precisely how. Maritain spoke of Psichari from such a reserve of memory, and with such intensity of feeling, that he had to hold himself constantly in check for fear of going far beyond the questions I was asking in my relative ignorance.

What he said was not the mere rehearsal of memory. He reiterated the fact that Ernest Psichari's adventure lay beyond his reach and comprehension. He minimized his own role in his friend's life and deliberately turned aside all the human and historical explanations. Since that first meeting at Meudon, I never saw Jacques's face so docile to the inner spirit. It became incandescent. The example of Psichari was an absolute for him, a pure example of God's entrance into a human being.

As soon as I brought up the name of Charles Péguy, I realized I had unwittingly broken the spell. The actual expression on Maritain's face did not alter. We were still within the framework of the same problem of God's intervention in the existence of a man, but in this new case the resisting will of a man had been stronger. Péguy was close to Maritain's heart—I never doubted that—but he had been difficult. In Psichari's case the human drama had been resolved, and had changed into what Maritain called the divine drama. In Péguy's case the human drama had continued, always appropriating more depth from the life of prayer, but never completely absorbing or converting the stubbornness of the writer.

As young men, Maritain and Psichari together came under the influence of Charles Péguy. They became his friends and learned from him, the peasant (the man who had never known how to sit in an armchair), the lessons on the dignity of work and labor. Maritain introduced Péguy to his mother, Madame Geneviève Favre, who became Péguy's best friend and guide. Every Thursday, for approximately two years, Péguy took lunch with Madame Favre in her apartment on the rue de Rennes, in company with her son Jacques and his friend Ernest. Maritain listened to Péguy and learned much from his constant discussion of the people (*le peuple*) and the theme that no political crisis is ever separated from the religious crisis.

Several years later, during World War II, Maritain came to Yale while I was teaching there to deliver a series of lectures on education. I invited him to dinner at Trumbull College where I was resident fellow, and invited also my chairman, Henri Peyre, who was anxious to meet him. The three of us ate at a small table in the college dining room. At one point Professor Peyre brought up the subject of Péguy. Very fervently, and with some justification, Peyre urged Maritain to write a book on Péguy, by saying there was a great need for such a book and that Maritain was the Frenchman best able to write it. Maritain closed the discussion by saying to Peyre—and there was sadness on his face and in his words—"That book I will never write" (*Ce livre-là je ne l'écrirai jamais*).

Let me return now to the Meudon days. When I was leaving Jacques on that first semiformal, semischolarly visit, he said to me, "I know you have met my niece Eveline Garnier, of whom Raïssa and I are very fond. Come with her, whenever you wish, on any Sunday afternoon, when we receive our friends, here at Meudon. Eveline knows almost everyone who comes on Sundays. She will introduce you and guide you."

I went several times, always hoping that I would at least see Jean

Cocteau, Julien Green, Marc Chagall, Georges Rouault. I never did see them at Meudon. I became, thanks to Eveline, a semifamiliar face to Jacques and Raïssa and Véra (Raïssa's sister) on those Sunday afternoons. Once Raïssa took me aside and said, "I want you and Eveline to stay for supper tonight. We always invite five or six friends to stay on, after the crowd has left."

Eveline had told me about that tradition and had promised me that one Sunday night I would be invited to stay. She had said there was usually one guest of honor who became the center of attention. The star that night was Henri Ghéon, a writer of religious plays. He had just returned from a visit to Jerusalem, and during the first part of supper he spoke of Jerusalem and announced that for dessert we were to have grapefruit he had brought from Jerusalem for Jacques and Raïssa. Véra, who supervised the supper, was especially delighted to have the dessert miraculously provided.

When talk about Jerusalem grapefruit subsided, Ghéon revealed a much more dramatic announcement, so serious that it shocked all of us who were assembled around the table. That morning— it was April 17, 1938, Easter morning—the wife of André Gide, Madeleine, had died. Ghéon had learned the news before it had been officially announced. I can still remember the hush that fell over that group of friends. Jacques bowed his head. He was the first to articulate what was, I imagine, in everyone's mind: "What change will this death bring about in André Gide?" It might easily —given all the circumstances of Gide's life, given the piety of Madeleine Gide, and the estrangement in that marriage, given the day itself, Easter—provoke a major change in Gide.

During the rest of the meal, until all of us left to return to Paris, and during the train ride, conversation continued to center on Madeleine Gide's death. The news appeared in the papers the next morning. The meaning of the drama behind the death was analyzed in countless articles and books during the next three or four months, as only the French analyze such matters.

The discussions that evening in Meudon, stimulated by Henri Ghéon's announcement in the presence of Jacques Maritain, represented for me, still a "French major" in an American university, an impressive page in the history of French literature.

In 1943, in the midst of the war, an ardent group of friends of
Jacques Maritain gathered at the Waldorf-Astoria Hotel in New
York to celebrate his sixtieth birthday. I was impressed not so much
by the large number of people who attended the luncheon as by
the variety of types of people who spoke on that occasion words
of homage and felicitation. There were, among others, a woman
journalist (Anne Freemantle), a college president, a Jewish painter
(Marc Chagall), a Catholic priest. That day was a celebration of
Jacques as friend rather than as philosopher or teacher or writer.

My thoughts that day turned back to Meudon, the gathering
place of friends on Sunday afternoons. The living room was always
crowded with Dominicans, poets, philosophy students, dramatists,
painters, *grandes dames*. The conversation always seemed to be about
art. On the walls the pictures by Severini and Chagall and the
sketch of Baudelaire helped perhaps to direct the conversation in
those channels.

This theme of art and poetry brings me to the last phase of my rec-
ollections, my memories of Jacques: the war years he spent largely
in New York in his apartment at 30 Fifth Avenue.

Those years in New York and later in Princeton were to culminate in the writing of *Creative Intuition in Art and Poetry* (1953), a
book that was to call upon American and English poets as well as
French poets. In the earlier works on aesthetics—*Art et scolastique,
Frontières de la Poésie*, and especially *Réponse à Jean Cocteau* (1926)—
Maritain developed a doctrine close to Baudelaire's *Correspondances*
and to the writings of Swedenborg. This doctrine might be defined
in this way: the spiritual is immanent in the real world, in what
we call reality. The interchange between the material world and
the spiritual world is constant, the one revealing the other, the one
standing as sign of the other.

Those artists so constantly admired and studied by Maritain—
poets like Baudelaire and Rimbaud, novelists like Léon Bloy and
Mauriac, the dramatist Cocteau, the composers Satie and Stravin-
sky—seemed to have for the philosopher one theme, one approach
in common: the incomprehensibleness of sin. The lives as well as

the literary exercises of these writers were tragic for Maritain. He watched them on their tightropes in the glare of the circus, and learned from their acrobatics and from their courage some aspects of the meaning of our civilization today.

During the war years I was at Yale, and I was able to come to New York whenever Jacques needed help in the translation of essays or lectures. He was working hard on English in those years, trying to write and lecture directly in English. Those visits were largely language lessons and revisions of some of the translations already done which he wanted to change. The one I liked best was *Le mystère d'Israël*, which ultimately became part of the book *Ransoming the Time* (1941).

During the fifties I was at Bennington College in Vermont, but taught also at the New School for Social Research, and therefore came to New York for two nights every week. The study of English and American poetry was Jacques's delight, almost his indulgence. Once I reminded him that Mallarmé had studied English in order to read Poe, and pointed out that he was studying English in order to read Eliot. He had met Eliot briefly at Princeton where he had also met Allen Tate. Behind these two poets whose work he was reading was a third man, also at Princeton, once my colleague at Bennington: Francis Fergusson, a careful reader of Maritain who was to write one of the most penetrating reviews of *Creative Intuition*.

At the end of our hard sessions on translations and linguistics, Maritain would turn to a few lines of Eliot and read them and ask me to read them out loud. He was curious about Eliot, curious about the depth of religious feeling in the poems. Once he asked me a question, an unusual kind of question for him to ask: "I have heard that you studied with Eliot. Would you say he is a religious man?" Rather than answering that question directly, I told Jacques the story of the Tuesday morning mass in the Cowley Fathers' chapel.

When I finished I noticed with some surprise that tears were rolling down his cheeks. He recovered quickly, smiled, and said: "I am going to tell you a story about myself, a comparable story. The first year that President Hutchins invited me to give a course at

the University of Chicago, I made arrangements to attend the earliest mass each morning at the Cathedral of the Holy Name. One
morning after I received communion, I must have had the same
experience, the same need that Eliot had and which you described.
I stretched out, face down, at the altar rail. There were only a few
people, and they had gone back to their seats. It was dark in the
church. A janitor came by and kicked me in the side, saying, 'We
don't allow drunks in this church.' He forced me to get up."

Of all the Eliot poems Jacques studied he was most strongly
attracted to *Ash-Wednesday*; that was the poem he was the most
anxious to discuss—in particular the last eleven lines of the poem.
During two of our sessions he asked me to read those eleven lines
to him. He would say this about them:

> In those lines I hear the beauty of pure sound, such as the *poètes
> maudits* strove to create. The words are so clear. It is a chant, a
> ritualistic chant which we don't really have in the French lan-
> guage.

At the end of one of the readings, I asked him in pedantic fashion,
"Do you recognize the line from Dante?" Rather than saying "yes,"
he quoted the line in Italian:

> En la sua voluntade è nostra pace.

I tried, on a few of the New York visits when there was time to
look at poetry, to interest Jacques in Hart Crane, in *The Bridge*, in
particular, Crane's long poem on America. I felt Jacques might find
stimulating the presentation of the cultural myth in the second part
of the poem, "Ave Maria," where Crane attempts to bridge the Old
World and the New. Crane's rather laborious reading of Baudelaire, and his even more laborious reading of Rimbaud, interested
Jacques, but by then Princeton was taking him away from New
York and the Brooklyn Bridge. At Princeton he came under the
strong influence of Allen Tate and Francis Fergusson, and accepted,
too readily, I think, their belief that *The Bridge*, a major American
poem, was also a major failure. Their theory stated that the myth
behind the poem was inadequate, insufficient to sustain its length.
This theory seems to be reflected in *Creative Intuition*. I felt defeated

in this effort of mine because I did not share Tate and Fergusson's conviction with respect to Crane's poem.

Jacques Maritain came in his turn to enter what Péguy called "an eternal concert." The man who today would speak of appearance and reality must speak the language of ancient Greece. He who would speak of belief in one God and of temporal justice must speak the language of Israel. He who would speak of the Fall and the Redemption of man will have to speak the language of the Christian Church.

Maritain's language sounded strange to men of this day—as strange as the language of other metaphysicians sounded to men of their day. But he who henceforth would speak of theocentric humanism or humanism of the Incarnation, of the hidden reserved sacramental power of the people, of the meaning of Christian freedom, will have to speak the language of Maritain.

CHAPTER 3

Remembering Noémi Renan

16, rue Chaptal

From the day of my arrival at 16, rue Chaptal, the home of Madame Noémi Renan, I was curious about the house itself, about its quaintness and its history. As soon as I had become accustomed to my part of the house—a very small bedroom and a small parlor where I worked at a large table—and for as long as I lived in that house during two winters in the middle thirties before World War II broke out, I continued to ask Mme Renan about the house during lunch and dinner when we were alone at the dining room table.

On this particular topic I had to ask the questions. On other topics, often related to the house, and because they were almost always on French literature and history, Mme Renan would speak easily and at length. The details about the house touched on more personal, more intimate subjects, and I soon realized that there I had to be more guarded and more willing to forgo total knowledge. The deeper dramas were not divulged. They were hinted at. The expression on her face told me then to move to some other topic.

If during lunch she avoided a direct answer to one of my awkward questions, she might, after dinner that night when I occasionally joined her in the large parlor for an hour of further talk, revive the question herself and add a bit more information about it. She never forgot those matters I often inadvertently brought up.

They stirred her memory, and she answered what she felt she could answer to her young American friend who would never comprehend the whole story and all the other stories she held in her heart and mind.

There were still faint traces on her face of a beautiful young girl. For both meals she dressed in simple, impeccable fashion as if I were a guest and not merely a boarder in her house studying the documents she gave me about her son, Ernest Psichari, the subject of my doctoral dissertation. Over her shoulders and covering her bosom there was usually a light shawl at lunch, or a collar of flat jet beads at dinner. She tempered the brilliance of the beads with a wisp of black net placed over the brief space of flesh at her neck. The unhealthy flush of old age in both cheeks contrasted with the pallor of her face and its heavy, abundant flesh. Her face had such an inquisitive, comprehending gaze that the shades of softness in her eyes were constantly being abandoned for shadows of intelligence, ideas, facts.

I looked forward to each meal and to the conversation that stimulated me and informed me about many matters. And I grew to believe that she too looked forward to the meals and our talk together. She seldom asked me questions about my life in America because her mind had become the past—her memories of the past which she rehearsed with me. I realized soon that Mme Renan was supreme in speech, in rhetoric, in the simple capacity of prolonging any theme far beyond its deserved profundity by the number of words and sentences she could deploy. She outwinded me easily in every conversation, no matter what the topic.

When I first learned that the house had been built by Ary Scheffer in 1830, I had to find out who he was: a French painter born in Dordrecht, Holland, in 1785. He had begun painting at the age of twelve and showed such talent that his mother decided that only Paris would allow her son to develop his gift. He was French at heart and chose, when the time came, Montmartre for his house and his studio. The site, 16, rue Chaptal, was not far from the noisy Pigalle section of Montmartre, but none of the noise ever reached the house built at the end of a passage (*une allée*), originally a carriage drive lined with trees and lilac bushes. It was, and still is, a charming provincial house with a short outside stairway going up to the main entrance. Below the first floor is a basement kitchen, where Esther, an expert cook and a very kind woman, prepared our meals and carried them up to the dining room.

I could see through a low window the copper warming pans (*bassinoires*) and the huge fish kettles (*poissonnières*) decorating the kitchen and testifying to what must have been a more than comfortable middle-class existence during the Restoration.

Each morning Esther carried my breakfast tray to my bedroom, the first room on the right on entering the hall from the outside stairway. The dining room was exactly opposite my room. Behind the dining room was a large parlor where Mme Renan sat each evening for an hour or two before retiring to her upstairs bedroom. Beside the large parlor was a small parlor reserved for my use and my work whenever I lived in Ary Scheffer's house.

The narrative of one hundred years, 1830 to the mid-1930s, provided me, thanks to Mme Renan's conversations, with stories of history and politics, the Restoration, the Dreyfus Affair, young Ernest Renan meeting, in this very house where we talked, the niece of the painter Cornélie Scheffer whom he married. Their child was Noémi Renan, the lady I ate with each day and who instructed me, in fragments, about Ary Scheffer, his house, his niece, his paintings, his despair over the Revolution of 1848, his friends who came to his house: Chopin, Liszt, Gobineau, Tocqueville, Ingres, Turgenev, Lamartine, Thierry. All of those names, and others less famous today, passed before me, not like ghosts but like strong personalities. The name that held first place, mentioned in some way or other every day, was the name of the father, Ernest Renan.

I had studied some of Renan's works at Harvard and was well aware of his importance as an historian, philologist, and literary stylist. In a totally false way I opposed in my mind the two names of Renan and Psichari, the venerable famous grandfather and the far less famous grandson, killed in 1914 in Belgium.

The younger Ernest was the reason for my being in that house. During the first winter I examined his letters and notebooks in order to document my thesis; the second winter, when the thesis had been written and accepted, I began to pay more attention to

Ernest Renan of Brittany. With the slightest encouragement on my part, Mme Renan spoke of her father. The tragedy of her son's death and his religious conversion were, I believe, deliberately put aside in the conversation during our meals. Ernest Renan was, after all, the major eminence in the family. The house at 16, rue Chaptal was the site of his courtship of Cornélie Scheffer. In speaking of the courtship of her father and mother, Noémi Renan made it into a love story, which indeed it was.

At times she referred to the energetic youthfulness of her two sons, Ernest and Michel, both killed in World War I, of the diminished glory of Ary Scheffer, and of the historical importance of his house where she lived. But her genuine eloquence was always reserved for her father. I know now that she was right in her preference, although I fought it in my own mind as we ate and talked.

Her background was Protestant. Her husband, Jean Psichari, a philologist and professor of modern Greek, was Greek Orthodox. Her son Ernest was a convert to the Catholic Church. The story of his conversion, related in his four books, was in the Paris press inevitably contrasted with the story of his grandfather leaving the seminary and renouncing the vocation of priest when he had lost his early faith.

Mme Renan and I never directly spoke of any theological matters. The closest we came to theology was Renan's philosophical, historical, and philological interests and attitudes toward the Catholic Church. The books we referred to the most often were *La vie de Jésus*, *Saint Paul*, and *Marc Aurèle*. I brought back into the conversation whenever I thought I could my favorite book by Renan, one of the last he wrote, *Souvenirs d'enfance et de jeunesse*, because there I had read of the boy Ernest falling in love with a little girl, Noémi, who died. It was the first sorrow in his life. I remembered the sentence where Renan wrote that if he ever had a daughter, he would call her Noémi. Only a few years after reading that sentence and being deeply moved by the autobiographical work, I was sitting each day in Paris at the dining room table and speaking with that Noémi.

How fortunate that we had no arguments about theology! How wise she was to emphasize her father's love and respect for the person of Jesus, and never once to criticize her son for turning away from Renan's convictions and revindicating the Church by his conversion! I felt at times in the midst of Church history but without any of the all too familiar elements of belligerency. Mme Renan's serenity reflected her father's serenity. She preferred to remind me of Renan's visits to that house and to Ary Scheffer. The historian Augustin Thierry had introduced the young scholar to the painter and thus to the painter's niece, Cornélie.

It was not easy in those days to pay court to a young girl. The Scheffers received their friends regularly on Friday evenings. Ernest Renan became an assiduous guest. At first it was impossible to see Cornélie alone. One Friday evening he announced to the group of friends seated in the large parlor that he was writing an article on the death of Augustin Thierry for *Le Journal des Débats*. Cornélie expressed the desire to see the article before it was printed. He sent her the article with a short note (*Mademoiselle . . . vos désirs sont des ordres . . . je vous transmets les deux chiffons que voici*). Cornélie was not unaware of the partially concealed emotion in the note.

The request for Cornélie's hand in marriage did not come immediately. Another drama was taking place in the rue Val-de-Grâce where Ernest lived with his sister, Henriette, who at first opposed the idea of the marriage. She believed there was too much disparity between the worldliness of the Scheffers and the simple peasant background of the Renans. Henriette forced her brother to declare he would not see Cornélie again. His chagrin was so evident that Henriette repented and came one night to the rue Chaptal to announce to Ernest's fiancée that the sister was restoring her brother's happiness. It was the spring of 1856 and the renascence of a love that was never belied.

Mme Renan ended that little story by saying that it was because of the drama between the rue Val-de-Grâce, close to the boulevard Saint Michel, and the rue Chaptal, close to the boulevard de Clichy, that she was here today in the house of Ary Scheffer. When her father first came to the house, two years before the marriage, he was a timid young man. By the time of the marriage he was already making headway toward glory. The marriage was celebrated on September 13, 1856, first in a Protestant church (le temple de l'Oratoire) and then in a Catholic church (Saint-Germain l'Auxerrois). As a footnote to her story Noémi Renan added that some years after the meeting between Ernest and Cornélie the house was rejuvenated by visits of Anatole France, and still later by the passionate discussions of Charles Péguy.

For my old friend, the house at 16, rue Chaptal was primarily the peaceful refuge where her father found his happiness.

I remember the first time when she suggested at the end of dinner that I sit with her for a brief spell in the parlor. I had wanted to do this, but had hesitated for fear of tiring her with more conversation. I watched her walk to the table lamp to light it. A wall light at the farther end gave only a feeble illumination. There, concentrated on the table with its neatly piled copies of *La Revue des deux mondes* and on the large figure bending down beside it, a rich glow from under the brocaded shade fell steadily and—as it seemed to me—slowly, in order to correspond to the measured movements of Mme Renan as she felt her way into the chair next to the table.

The room seemed large to me, overcrowded with furniture and souvenirs of something more than one hundred years. Heavy curtains at her right blocked off the dining room. We could hear the clinking of wine glasses as Esther cleared the table. "I am too often alone in this large room," she said to me on that first after-dinner visit. "It is so filled with the past, with the past that is dead, that on some evenings when Esther retires early, I feel I have died also."

I mentioned to her the rue Bonaparte where I had gone on an errand that afternoon and said how much I loved that section of Paris. I caught myself speaking as if I were a Parisian: "I deliberately got off the bus at the Institut and walked down the entire rue Bonaparte to the Place Saint Germain. It was just turning dark. The art shops were all lighted, and, since it was already a week from New Year's, the shopkeepers were taking out of the windows their most prized pieces and putting back the familiar ones we see all year."

She apparently listened to me, but I knew that inwardly she was formulating her own opinion. "It is a beautiful part of Paris," she said, "but has always seemed to me too sad, too grave. There is a monotony in all those streets between the Seine and the boulevard Saint-Germain. Even the church itself is colder and more austere than other churches of Paris."

By this time in our growing friendship I knew that her gods were science, democracy, and beauty. Truth was redefined with each century, and man attained his dignity by searching for it. I always feared that she would consider me hostile to her beliefs, and I often spoke of the gratitude I felt for the vigorous way in which she revived her past for me. When she apologized that the room in which we sat was a museum with its family photographs, the table with its heavy lamp, the divan so narrow and hard that one could only sit on it straight and uncomfortably, I insisted that it was much more for me than a museum. I pointed out to her the six tall volumes of Renan's *Les Origines du Christianisme*, preserved behind glass. They were bound in green leather with gold lettering. And I would say to her that each time I looked at them through the glass, I felt urged to continue with my own work.

Tréguier: The Spell of Renan's Brittany

Before I returned to 16, rue Chaptal for a second winter visit and work period in Paris, I spent, on an intervening summer in France, a week in Tréguier, Renan's birthplace in Brittany, inland in the province but not very far from the sea. I had already seen some of the coastline, Quiberon and Perros-Guirec, but I had wanted above all to see the town of Tréguier and visit the house itself where Renan was born, which was being restored thanks to the efforts of his two granddaughters, Henriette Psichari and Corrie Siohan. Through the writings of Renan, and especially the novels of Pierre Loti, I was familiar with the gray sky of Brittany, the granite color of its houses and the slate of its roofs. I had crossed once on a patrol boat (*une vedette*) to the rose-gray island of Bréhat, and from there in the evening watched the lighthouses blinking against a foggy sky.

The center of the town is the cathedral with the purest ogives (pointed arches) I have ever seen. The interior of the cathedral has the warmest natural light of any church I have ever visited. The main attraction of the small garden close to the cathedral is the statue of Ernest Renan whose heavy bronze belly seems to sink down on to the bench where he sits. Mme Renan told me the statue was inaugurated by the anticlerical political figure Emile Combes at the beginning of the century when he was proposing the law of separation of church and state. She said that during the inaugural address his voice was covered up by the cathedral bells. One hundred meters from that garden, on the street now called la rue Ernest Renan, one comes upon the house, the site today of a museum and pilgrimage.

On my first visit Henriette Psichari showed me the entire house from top to bottom and introduced me to the devoted guardian, Mme Jeanne Filous, who, on subsequent visits, demonstrated to me considerable learning about the beginnings of Renan's life. Her piety was fervent. Formerly a baker in Louannec, she had become one of those faithful servants who belong to the family they serve.

The house is a humble peasant dwelling which was built in the first years of the seventeenth century. Renan was born there in 1823. In 1845 he left the seminary and gave up his intention of becoming a priest. Because of the scandal caused by this rejection of the priesthood, his mother had to leave Tréguier for Saint-Malo. Renan did not return to his native town until 1882. It was then a triumphant return. For many years the house was rented, but the cult of Renan was maintained by the Psichari family and by Michel Psichari's marriage to the daughter of Anatole France and by their son Lucien Psichari. Renan and France had similar philosophical and spiritual beliefs.

In 1923, the centenary celebration of Renan's birth, the house as a modest museum was opened to the public. The ground floor is one large room which had served as both kitchen and bedroom. There are portraits of Renan, autographs, caricatures, and his academician's sword. I looked into his address book of later years and saw there the names of Michelet, Guizot, and Monseigneur Dupanloup (the priest who protected him until the publication of *La Vie de Jésus*).

Of all the relics in that room I was most attracted to Henriette's green shawl. She wore it whenever she called on her brother in

Paris—a modest shawl which in the words of Renan himself "had sheltered her proud poverty" (*ce châle qui avait abrité sa fière pauvreté*).

All of these objects are still today in the musée Renan in Tréguier which was given to the French government by the granddaughters. The house has been restored without changing the original forms. The fireplace has been rebuilt with the rose-colored granite from the Ile Bréhat.

From her memories Mme Renan spoke particularly of the third floor where there is a small room warmly illuminated by daylight. It was young Ernest's room, with a view over a good deal of the city and the river where the incoming tide was always visible. The small desk is there on which he wrote his school exercises, and the notebooks themselves are carefully grouped together, beside the prize books won every year. I remember especially Fénelon's *Télémaque*, his history prize in the *cinquième* grade.

As Henriette Psichari showed me the treasures of the house, she spoke at the same time of her work on the new edition of her grandfather's complete works, to be published by Calmann-Lévy. The ten volumes were published between 1947 and 1961. Of all her scholarly works, I like best her edition of *La Prière sur l'Acropole* (1956), the Renan text that still figures in the lycée program, and the text by which, I imagine, he is best remembered. At her birth in 1884 she was given the name of Euphrosyne, but with her first publication she adopted the name of Henriette, in memory of Renan's sister. At her death in 1972, she was a very old lady, older than her mother Noémi Renan at her death in 1943.

I listened through many years to these ladies, mother and daughter, who preserved very special memories of Ernest Renan. Noémi's memories were sentimental and loving. Henriette's were a veritable cult for the political and philosophical ideas and the scholarly achievements of her grandfather.

Ernest Renan (1823–1892)

During the past decade of my life all traces of the resentment I may have once felt toward Renan have disappeared. I have returned to reading pages of his *Averrhoès* and especially of his *Saint Paul*. My friendship at Duke with my colleague in the Divinity School, W. D. Davies, may be one of the reasons for this renewed appreciation. W. D., as he is called, also wrote at the beginning of his career a study of Saint Paul, and today he is writing and editing a history of Israel in several volumes for Cambridge University Press. There are several parallels in the life story of Renan and in the very rich scholarly career of Professor Davies.

Ernest Renan bore the name of a Breton saint who lived as a hermit. Like many Bretons he was haunted throughout his life by religion and by the sea. These have been called the two voices of Brittany. His father, a sea captain, died when Ernest was five. He was raised by two women, his mother and his sister Henriette. His intuitive sensitivity, so different from the more provocative Chateaubriand, may be traced to them. They knew that Ernest was promised to God, and they were determined that he would become one of God's priests.

His sister secured a scholarship for him at the Paris seminary of Saint Nicolas du Chardonneret. The director, M. Dupanloup, who later became "Monseigneur," presided over Renan's early studies and was fully aware of the boy's powers. After a year at the seminary of Issy (1892–93), he moved to the important Paris seminary of Saint-Sulpice where he studied Hebrew under Abbé Le Hir. There his first doubts assailed him. At the age of twenty he put off receiving the tonsure and minor orders. At twenty-two he refused the subdiaconate and left the seminary (1854).

At one of his assistant teaching posts (la pension Crouzet) he met and befriended Marcelin Berthelot (1827–1907), destined to become an eminent scientist and political leader. After receiving a degree (*une licence*) in literature and one in science, he won an *agrégation* in philosophy, and then began a lifelong study of philology. Later he claimed that the study of historical criticism (*la critique historique*), especially Hebrew philology, destroyed his faith. He wrote on the Semitic languages, and, urged by Berthelot, wrote a book on modern science which he did not publish until two years before his death, *L'Avenir de la Science*. This book stresses the belief that the authority for man is human nature and not divine revelation. Man's reason is the power that will reform society by means of rational science.

In the middle of the century Renan did considerable research in the Vatican Library, and at the same time he discovered the beauty of Italy, the light of its skies and its flowers. There he worked on Averrhoès, the Arabian philosopher of the twelfth century whose writings were condemned by the University of Paris and by the pope as being materialist and pantheist. This was the subject of Renan's thesis that made him a doctor at twenty-nine (1852): *Averrhoès et l'averrhoisme*—a provocative thesis for an exseminarian to write. His marriage in 1856 marked the definitive break with the priesthood.

Renan's style of writing is both scholarly and priestly. He remained a Breton, nostalgic for his native province. All of his writings are based on his belief that the Semites invented monotheism and transmitted it to the Aryans. As a student of Hebrew, he looked upon Christianity as a Jewish fact. The origins of Christianity, according to Renan, are not in the writings of the Fathers of the Church, but in the apocryphal books of Jewish origin.

As I read Renan, I began to understand for the first time that history is in reality the history of religions, and that the religious sentiment is the profoundest and the most permanent instinct in man. That is why I renewed my contact with Renan, not only in the thirties on the rue Chaptal, but in these last few decades of my life.

In Syria, in 1860–61, when Renan was on an archeological mission, his sister Henriette, who accompanied him, died from a fever. On his return to Paris, at the age of thirty-nine, he was given a professorship at the Collège de France, to teach the Hebraic, Chaldean, and Syriac languages. In his inaugural lesson he spoke of Jesus as an "incomparable man" (*homme incomparable*). Five days later his course was suspended (1862) as being an offense against Christian belief. Attacks against Renan were even stronger the following year (1863) when he published *La Vie de Jésus*. Renan wanted to be only a scholar and an historian.

In this controversial book he wrote a pastoral story treating Jesus as a handsome man unable to keep people from loving him, unable not to perform miracles in the midst of children and people acclaiming him. Then, later, in the third volume of the *Histoire des origines du christianisme* (1869), he wrote the story of Saint Paul whom he looked upon as a fanatic able to set fire to a village and massacre the inhabitants. Still later, when he was sixty, he wrote the story of Marcus Aurelius (*Marc Aurèle*), a courageous emperor who wanted the good for all men.

One day, at the rue Chaptal, in summarizing some of her stories, Noémi Renan said to me that her father wanted to be the spiritual director of his time. She used the words *directeur de conscience*. In accord with his chemist friend Berthelot, he wanted criticism and philosophy to protect science. In his own unique way Renan remained the Breton priest independent of his bishop. He distrusted religious symbols, which he considered perishable. The study of philology was a kind of prayer for Renan, as the study of chemistry was a prayer for Berthelot.

Part of me responded strongly to these thoughts, which were always offset in Noémi Renan's conversation by the picture she gave of social and political Renan. She seemed proud when she said that her father, at the end of the Second Empire, was often a guest of la Princesse Mathilde (1820–1904), daughter of Jérôme, brother of Napoleon Bonaparte. Her Paris salon was one of the most brilliant at the end of the century.

Renan deeply felt the disaster of the Franco-Prussian War. He became almost a pontiff during the Third Republic as he developed in his writings the concept of the French nation. Elected to the Académie Française in 1878, in 1883 he was made administrator of the Collège de France from which Napoleon III had ostracized him.

Some called him the Montaigne of the Third Republic, as he refused to affirm anything in such sentences as, *qui sait si la vérité n'est pas triste?* (who knows if truth is not sad?). He belongs understandably to the line of doubters that goes from Montaigne to Anatole France and to André Gide. In one of his most celebrated texts, his *Prière sur l'Acropole*, constantly referred to in my presence at lunch and dinner, Renan claims that good and evil, pleasure and pain, the beautiful and the ugly, reason and madness, have as many indiscernible shadings as those we see on the neck of a dove.

Prayer on the Acropolis

The references Noémi Renan made to the *Prière sur l'Acropole* were, as I remember, fragments of quotations. I always recognized them. The phrases are so memorable—as are the lines of a great poem—that I knew them without having literally memorized them. I had read the text first in *Souvenirs d'enfance et de jeunesse*, but passages from it had been used in various ways in general courses I had taken in college on nineteenth-century French literature.

After the second winter with Noémi Renan and the summer with Henriette Psichari in Perros-Guirec and Tréguier, I returned to the text when I was at Yale during the four war years when there was no chance of reaching France. There the *Prière* became an experience of reading for me. During the one conversation I had with Henri Focillon, ill in his room at the Taft Hotel in New Haven, he spoke of that page because he wanted to speak of Noémi Renan whom he admired. In a way he was testing me out, trying me out to see if I could respond, not so much to the ideas in the *Prière* as to the music of those lines and to their images. Then he would forget to test me as he himself was caught up by the rhythm and the beauty of the lines. "A jewel," he called it, "shining forth in the midst of all the memories of a philosopher."

Such words from such a wise man urged me back once again to the text and I began again marveling at the resonance that I heard between the text and me the reader. I could easily find reasons for that resonance, reasons in my own religious background and in my study of French, but I never discovered all the reasons, because they would be from all of my life—the years I remembered and the years I had forgotten. Alone with that text as I read it out loud, I experienced, without totally understanding, the magical power of words. My vocation of teacher of French literature appeared to me then to be a force I would never have been able to deny or refuse. It confirmed me in every way—in my search for belief, for beauty in literature, for ideas that would stimulate me and that I could understand in the experiences of my own life.

The role of the text was revealed to me at 16, rue Chaptal. Noémi Renan told me something of the long history of the text; that history years later was written carefully and lucidly by Henriette Psichari in her edition, *La Prière sur l'Acropole et ses mystères* (1956, Edition CNRS).

Behind every work of art there is a man, and our knowledge of that man enriches his work without destroying it. This conviction guides me in the three courses I now give at Duke University and elsewhere on Dante, Rimbaud, and Proust.

La Prière is made up of arguments for and against Christianity and arguments for and against Greek civilization. Renan reiterates many times that no one religion possesses all truth. Christianity neglected the rules of Reason which the Greeks followed. The temple on the Acropolis in Athens is more reasonable than the huge Gothic cathedrals of France. Greek philosophy is incomplete because of its reliance on Reason and because it speaks to an elite. Christian churches, with their liturgy and songs, gave to the congregations filling cathedrals on holy days the sensation and the feeling of the divine.

The subjective parts of the *Prière* meant the most to me and still do today as I mingle in my mind Renan's theme of childhood and my own memories of childhood and their hours spent in a church. At the prayer's beginning, Renan tells us that he came late to the threshold of the Greek mysteries: *J'arrive tard au seuil de tes mystères.* More than for the typical young Athenian, Renan had needed endless research and endless reflection to comprehend the simple true beauty of the Greeks (*ô beauté simple et vraie*). He was born on the shore of a dark sea bristling with rocks, forever beaten by storms (*une mer sombre, hérissée de rochers, toujours battue par les orages*).

With these memories of Brittany, so different from the memories of a young Athenian, he speaks of his priests coming originally from Palestine, holy men who taught him how God (Cronus) created the world and how his Son spent some time on the earth. Their temples are three times higher than Greek temples, but they fall into ruins at the end of four or five hundred years. Their builders did not follow the laws of reason. Those priests were wise holy men. (*Ces prêtres étaient sages et saints.*) Yet they attacked the son of Brittany when he wrote the life story of the young God who walked on the earth. They called him Evhémère, the Greek who in the third century B.C. humanized mythological characters.

Difficulties remained for Renan, habits of his mind that had to be changed, bewitching memories that had to be wrenched from his head. It was late in his life when he recognized perfect beauty (*Tard, je t'ai connue, beauté parfaite*). He ended his prayer with very simple and tragic words summarizing his thought: "Everything on this earth is symbol and dream" (*Tout n'est ici-bas que symbole et songe*). "The gods pass as man passes, and it would not be good for them to be eternal" (*Les dieux passent comme les hommes et il ne serait pas bon qu'ils fussent éternels*).

Since Renan wrote his *Prière*, how many young men like myself have held similar thoughts—at least temporarily or intermittently —and suffered from their search for truth because of the memories of their childhood coupled with their desire to break with the past? The *prière* is a prose poem, and today I can study it, recite it, and feel once more seduced by the harmonious balancing of its sentences.

CHAPTER 4

The Catalpa Tree

The scene is Chicago, my apartment on Woodlawn, the fourth year I taught at the university close by, and the date would be 1949–50. This story is not about my teaching or the university or the city of Chicago. But all of that is necessarily behind the story.

No, this story is about a catalpa tree and a young boy I saw standing under it. My apartment, on the second floor of what was once a single house, had a porch from which I could look down on this tree, the first of its kind I had ever observed closely and daily. I could see it too from the one window in my living room. I say "living room," which it was, but it was in fact the only room, with a bath and kitchenette attached. My bed at the end I blocked off with a screen. A stage set, my apartment on Woodlawn, which I altered by means of props according to the hours of day or night when I inhabited it. When students came or when a friend came to visit with me, I acted on the stage of that set using it judiciously, histrionically.

One day I had caught a glimpse of a slight figure under the catalpa tree, frail almost. It had disappeared very fast. Had I scared him away when he saw me looking at him? Yet he had been looking at me or for me, or looking at my porch or my window. Each of us must be curious about the other, but unwilling to be seen by the other. The second time I noticed him, he did not see me at first. I stood behind the curtain at my window and clearly saw the solemn face of a boy, nine or ten years old, an oval face resembling an angel's face I had often seen in Italian paintings. This boy, I repeated to myself, might be an angel in exile. I thought of the face of Rimbaud as described by Mallarmé in the letter he wrote to Rimbaud's mother, and as once sketched by Picasso. I immediately endowed this boy with important literary-artistic ancestry.

I turned my head aside at that moment to cough, and when I turned back three seconds later he was not there. How and where had he disappeared so fast? He must have noticed that I had seen him, and then, in keeping with the game that was being played, made off. The mystery of it all was still intact. That boy had vanished like a fox in tall grass. But there was no tall grass around the catalpa. There was only the shorn grass of the lawn, golden as stubble is in the rich light of late afternoon.

Was the scene fantasy or real? I set about inventing reasons for the boy's approach—so tentative an approach—and the stillness of his figure as he stood under the tree. Was he aware of my loneliness and then too timid to wait and speak? Did mere curiosity explain his moments of observation? A planned theft, perhaps? No, that was impossible. His face was too innocent for such a plot.

I could summon up only the vaguest recollection of details. His hair was fair and plastered to his forehead. He wore a school sweater partly opened on a gray shirt that stuck to him. He was not yet old enough for adolescence, and he was not young enough to have the prominent tummy of children. The features of his face were indistinct to me, although I did see a mildness about his eyes and mouth.

Once again he had disappeared from sight, and I could go back to my work which was spread out on the large table I used for both writing and eating.

As the morning wore on, and later in the day during the two classes I taught at the university, thoughts about the strange youngster forced other thoughts out of their usual place. The word "stranger" always calls up for me an element of the supernatural. Was he a messenger? A boy forced to obey an instinct that he himself did not understand? I was on the verge of inventing ludicrous hypotheses, of assigning to this lad a secret, perhaps sacred mission.

When the classes ended that day, I walked back to Woodlawn. I was at last free to imagine such explanations and began deriding myself.

On reaching my house, rather than going up the stairs to the front porch that led to the downstairs apartment as well as to my own, I took the path beside the house to prowl around the catalpa and see if I could make out the way by which that boy had escaped. I was eager to dissolve the strangeness of the entire episode, which in reality was nothing in itself, and which my imagination had blown up into a mystery story.

We saw one another at the same time, and I knew that his shock was as strong as mine at our coming finally face to face. He was standing under the tree. I stood just a few yards away from him, determined to hold him this time with a few questions.

I smiled and tried to speak as casually as I could. If he was frightened, I knew he would dart off once again.

"Hello, I was hoping you might come by again today. I have been wanting to speak with you."

The boy did not look startled, as I thought he might. He patted the thin trunk of the tree softly.

"Hello, sir." His voice was pitched lower than I expected it would be. "I come by here quite often after school lets out, and watch for you to come home. You teach at the University of Chicago, don't you?"

"Yes, I do. I am guessing now: are you about ten?"

"I'm eleven. Everyone takes me for younger. The boys make fun of me in school."

"It's your complexion, perhaps. The skin on your face looks like a newly washed plum. . . . That's meant to be a compliment."

"Thanks. I'll grow up some day, and look like a man."

There was a pause then. I became aware of his stillness. His body was very still, but his blue eyes had a bright intentness. I went on.

"It is good to be able to talk with you at last. What is your name, and where is your school?"

"Matthew Wall. School is on the other side of the Midway. I live there, on 63rd Street. It's better over here. And that is why I come. Ever since I have been seeing you, I am able to make up stories about what it must be to live over here. I heard a man once call this side of the Midway 'a city of books.' "

"That's a good phrase. All of us over here spend too much time with books. Do you like school?"

"I like some of the classes and a few of the teachers. What do you teach?"

"I teach literature—French literature mainly. Do you study French?"

"Next year. Then you and I could speak in French, do you think? I'd like that."

"That means you will become my friend. I have wanted to invite you inside, for a Coke or something cool."

"I guess not today. But some day soon. Thanks."

"Why do you come here? Let me say right away that I'm glad you do come."

"When I'm here, under this tree, I'm able to make up stories about the house, about you, and about other people in the house. You live alone, don't you?"

"Yes, I live alone, in an almost empty apartment. But what started it all—your coming here across the Midway?"

"One day I saw you walking away from the university. You were carrying that little suitcase you still have in your hand today. And I began wondering about you. I watched you go into the house, and then I saw you at the window upstairs, and I thought you were looking down at the tree."

"I guess this old tree is important to both of us. It's a catalpa tree. And this little 'suitcase' is called an attaché case."

"You're a teacher all right. I like learning new words. Catalpa tree. Attaché case. I'll try to remember them."

I felt already a closed circuit of sympathy. But in Matthew there was an inner intensity of avoidance and secrecy. Above all, there was a stillness about the boy that marked him out. I noticed how his gray shorts that matched his shirt were sticking to him with sweat.

"These fall days can be hot. Are you sure you don't want something cool to drink?"

"I'll come up some other day. I have so much to think about, now that we have spoken. I must get back to the bad side of the Midway."

During those few words we had exchanged, I believed I had seen the sign of pleasure on his face. But now, with the fatal word "Midway," the rose of happiness faded slowly from his cheeks.

I knew he couldn't be held back much longer and spoke then in what must have been a tone of resignation. "I tried to get you before, but you escaped into thin air. How do you move so fast?"

"I don't weigh as much as you. I pretend sometimes I'm a bird."

"What kind of bird?" I wanted to keep talking with him a bit longer.

"A small bird, I guess, small like me, and afraid when anyone comes near. . . . Are you afraid if people come close to you?"

"I used to be. Now in my life I don't see many people coming close. You are the only one, Matthew. And you haven't come very close so far. But you are not alone as I am. You have your parents."

"I live alone with my mother. But she is never there except at night when I'm asleep."

"Where is your father?"

"I don't have one. Do you have a boy of your own living somewhere else?"

"No."

We were skirting too close to big subjects, and I thought it better to close it off.

Matthew, too, must have felt this need, and he ended it all by saying, "I'll be back on Saturday, and I'll come up then. I never know what to do on Saturdays when there is no school."

"We'll find something to do. My house needs a boy like you."

He was off then, fast, in the narrow space between the two houses that lined the back of my yard. The afternoon sun slanted in from the tree. Suddenly there was a slight breeze from the lake that scattered light over the yard. I turned back to the front of the house. There was only one entrance to my apartment, only one stairway.

Because of that first brief talk with Matthew when so little was said and so much was implied, my apartment, when I entered it, appeared to me like an uninhabited island. No people were on that island, no houses, no smoke, no boats off the shore. Sweat had soaked my clothes. The Chicago heat was heavy and damp. I took a shower in my small bathroom, and as I dried myself with a large towel, I began enjoying my triumph. The meeting had been something like an achievement. Some of the mystery that had been plaguing me was being dissolved.

I worked steadily during the next two days on class preparations and on a book review I was writing. I gave very little thought to Saturday—perhaps because it seemed certain to me that a second meeting with Matthew would take place and it would be more comfortable, more relaxed than the first. I hoped that still more mystery would be dissipated.

They were, on the whole, silent days, save for the hours in the classroom with that ring of faces around me. The silence was easy because I felt borne on my triumph. Each afternoon the sun lay golden over half of my porch. A light breeze came in from the lake which reminded me that I was still on an island. But no longer quite alone. The slanting sunlight was real. There was also a strange invisible light of friendship—not the friendship of students and colleagues but that of a boy who had watched me and who was perhaps now thinking of me. Why? What did he want of me?

His face was now visible to me. It was a peaceful face. Egyptian, like the face I had seen on the coffin of Tutankhamen. Thick lips, eyes that closed easily, hair like tow or flax, which should have been black if he were really Egyptian. Because of the intruder—a welcome intruder—I felt, more acutely than I had in the past, my life without a child, without a son. Is that why the small figure under the catalpa had puzzled me at first, and then attracted me, as if he represented a plot to unravel? His words, "I don't have one," (a father) were the words I remembered. All his other words, by comparison, were trivial. I sensed that untouched within him were certain "dark" things.

Soon, when we reached the middle of October, the catalpa would lose its hundreds of leaves. Some of them would in time enrich the soil of my yard, and others would cover the Woodlawn street. It would become a slippery road when rain fell on those leaves.

Would it have been better if I had not spoken to the mysterious visitor? Before exchanging those words, I had grown to think of him as an emissary, an angel even. I too had made up stories that probably did not coincide with the truth. As the facts were revealed (he lived on the other side of the Midway), all would seem natural. Even his habitual winged flight would be explained—in fact, it was already being explained. Mystery, equivocation—let me leave all that in the texts of Stéphane Mallarmé. Here was a chance, one of the rare chances in my life (far too ordered by mysteries in books) to come face to face with a living being who represented my own being and that of an Egyptian pharaoh.

It was time to give up the commissioned article I was trying to do (for *Romance Philology*, the most unlikely of reviews for me), and consider a bigger work, a kind of novel, perhaps, if I was able to endure, to last through that part of it I would have to live.

From an early age I had tried to write, and by now, in my middle thirties, I had passed through various phases. After periods of slovenly work I had attempted more careful work, always looking for what I could do honestly. Could I at the end write a work of my own, with a minimum of slavish imitation? What I was imitating now was just a phrase or two, a few words that started me off, that seduced me. A point of departure, I called it. A flash, almost, igniting something that hurtled me far back in my memory.

Teaching French and literature kept me in contact with people younger than myself. I was not too old yet, but I was old enough to need contact with the young. An unknown boy had appeared and disappeared—twice, three times, or more. He was much younger than the fellows in my classes. I knew nothing of their early lives, and that is precisely what I had often wanted to know, in order to understand them better and teach them matters more relevant to their needs.

How isolated I had become! To change this situation, possibly, all that was needed was a young face that had looked up at my window—not really at me. He wanted the house, not me, I said to myself. Well, there is plenty of space here for a grown man and a young boy. My house is not haunted by my past, my own past and the past of my ancestors. . . . Rimbaud again, on the first page of *Mauvais sang*. Rimbaud himself and his other self. *Je est un autre.*

Matthew, so frail-looking, and yet so steadfast as long as he stood there looking. And I, too, stand now looking down at what I have been looking at all this year: the green patch of the yard and the tree with its leaves alive with every breeze, with every shift of the wind.

Creepers should be festooning that tree trunk. The island and I are very still. It is an uncommunicative island. No whirr of insects. Only silence. But the silence now has been shattered. I had seen a passing pallor on Matthew's face, and then I had seen a surge of blood change that pallor. When the leaves come fluttering down, will that end the story? After all, I am on a good island where I have seen flashes of light through the foliage.

Saturday came, and I had no notion as to the time Matthew might arrive. I put my house in order, worked an hour or two, and then set about preparing a lunch in case the boy came early. I really did not expect him until late afternoon. At eleven o'clock there was a knock on the door. I didn't believe it could be Matthew because the door downstairs is kept locked. It was Matthew, smiling, and explaining that the front door was open when he came to it. A man was sweeping the porch.

I welcomed him in, shook hands—he smiled at that gesture, but I think he liked it.

"I'm glad you came now. We can have lunch here if you can put up with a simple meal."

"Thanks, sir. I'd like to have lunch with you if it is not too much bother. I thought I should have waited until this afternoon, but I've been anxious to come. I woke up early and couldn't wait any longer."

"It's fine you're here. Let me get things ready and set the table. My one table, as you can see. Why don't you just prowl about and get accustomed to the place. You've been on the outside of things too long. We can talk back and forth as I warm up some soup I made yesterday."

The boy assumed an air of purpose as he began moving about my small quarters. There was not much to look at. I explained that it was a furnished apartment I had rented for the year. My own

furniture was in storage back east. He seemed interested in the ar-
rangement of the room: the large bed at one end somewhat hidden
by a screen, a sofa in the middle of the room that could pull out
into a bed, the proximity of my table to the porch where he had
seen me looking down at the catalpa and at him.

His light golden hair was tangled, and his tan skin glistened with
sweat. I suggested he wash up in the bathroom. He did—eagerly,
I thought. That was another spot in my establishment to explore.
When he came out, the food was ready—leek-potato soup and tuna
salad sandwiches, good ones with cut-up celery in them. I was
standing on the porch. He joined me there, and I pointed out a nest
of yellow jackets in one corner of the porch, high up. They had
given me no trouble and I often watched their activity, as deliberate
and routine as my own activities.

"It's good to have something alive close by. I don't have a cat or
dog or even goldfish."

He picked up then on my train of thought, and added, "or even
a boy like me."

"I have lots of boys and girls in my classes, but no boy as young
as you. My island home seems more civilized with you here."

"Island?" There was an opaque mad look in his eyes as he questioned the word "island." He was looking at me through the tangle
of fair hair.

"Yes, I guess I haven't told you about my imagining this place
where I live to be an island. And it's easy for me to imagine the
catalpa a forest where I'm utterly alone. Waiting to be rescued. Do
you feel like a rescuer, Matthew?"

I knew this to be an unusual declaration, but once again he picked
right up on it as we sat down in front of our bowls of soup. He
was in the habit of practicing his imagination as often as I was.

"I don't know what I could rescue you from, but I promise I'd
work hard at it."

A flash of honey-colored sunlight hit the floor beside the table
where we had been eating.

"What is this soup? It tastes good."

"It's leek soup. *Potage aux poireaux et aux pommes de terre,* as a
Frenchman would call it. It's a peasant soup, really, nutritious and

heavy. It's easy to make: you just chop up a few leeks and a few potatoes, and cook them for an hour in two quarts of water."

"I keep learning words as you talk to me. I like that. Out on the porch you said 'yellow jackets.' They looked like 'wasps' to me. And now 'leeks' which I'm eating. Would they be in the vegetable stores on 63rd Street?"

"You'll find them in stores that cater to people from Europe, from France and Italy."

I sensed then that he wanted to move on to more important matters. After all, he was piercing mysteries, as I was too in my own way.

"You know" (Matthew had almost a new voice as he spoke now), "I eat alone like you. My mother leaves food for me in the refrigerator, and I can make it into a meal. It's funny, when you think of it —you and me eating alone each day, with the Midway between us. When I watched you, or watched for you to come home, I imagined, among other things, my walking with you, or even eating with you as I'm doing right now. Was I crazy, do you think?"

"Well, I would say you weren't crazy because you're here, and about to have some applesauce. That's all I have for dessert."

Matthew knew I was trying to make everything seem simple and natural. And he refused to give up before pushing to the final point he wanted to make. I was not surprised when he made the point because he had prepared the way.

"Could you be my father? Would you ever consider being my father? It wouldn't have to mean that I'd live here with you. But I'd be able to see you from time to time, and you could help me learn new words. My mother doesn't really need me. She sees too many men now, and they don't want to have me around. I'm scared that she might marry one of them, and then what would become of me?"

These words made everything clearer to me. They threw light not only on Matthew's life but on my own.

I spoke then, without the slightest effort, from the deepest part of me. "I promise to do everything I can to make this possible, to help you, and to teach myself how to be a good father."

He came to me then, put his arms around my waist and his head on my chest. The promise was made and acknowledged. For the next hour we spoke of other matters, of school, of Chicago, of a boy's dream about the future, his own future and mine.

That night, alone in my apartment that had once been watched over by the boy with whom I had never spoken, I saw ahead of me my life richer than it had ever been, and governed by a purpose. Matthew would not be as much helped as I would be.

A week went by then without his appearing either under the tree or upstairs on my porch. After the tenth day had come and gone, I found the address of "Wall" on 63rd Street, and walked across the Midway one afternoon to make inquiries. The man in charge of the building told me the mother and son had moved out, in a great rush, to go to California. No forwarding address. "The wrong kind of mother for such a son. He used to take care of her rather than the other way around." The man seemed to know more than he wanted to say, more than I wanted to hear.

My first thought was: Matthew will write. He never did. I was a father without his son. This absence has been a dark thread, a dark mystery weaving throughout my life ever since. That fall season in Chicago, the leaves of the catalpa fell in large numbers soon after Matthew's flight, a flight I am confident he was forced to take. I have looked for him in the hundreds of students I have faced in the classroom, Matthew or someone resembling Matthew and needing a guide as much as I have needed someone to guide.

PART II

CHAPTER 5

The Story of Some Pictures

1938: Hall House, Old Bennington

In the late 1930s I lived for one of the school years in an apartment that had been constructed in the Hall House, one of the white-columned houses in Old Bennington, acquired by the college four miles away in North Bennington. It was my first real home, whose bare walls had depressed me during the fall term. I owned a clavichord but no pictures. That winter in Paris (Bennington College closes down every January and February) I was shown, in a favorite bookstore on the Boulevard Montparnasse, a reproduction of a large painting by Georges Rouault—*le vieux roi*—a hieratic King David, perhaps, glowing with reds and blacks and a jewelled crown. It was a silkscreen reproduction, a new process at that time. I felt it destined for my Old Bennington living room, and purchased it. This was the start, although it was just a reproduction, of a small collection of pictures I gathered from various sources during the next half century (1938–1987).

I had seen original Rouaults in Washington and Paris, read about the painter in Maritain's *Art et scolastique*, and associated him with the religious spirit in man. As spring came to Vermont in 1938 I lived with "King David," as I called the picture. By itself on a white wall facing the entrance to my apartment, it dominated my home, a more temporary home than I imagined it would be that spring.

The English actor Robert Speaight came to the college in March to give a reading of Eliot's poems and of scenes from his plays. Just a few weeks earlier in London I had seen him play the archbishop in *Murder in the Cathedral*, and I had met him briefly, thanks to a letter of introduction from Jacques Maritain. Speaight was the author of a biography of Georges Bernanos I had enjoyed reading.

It was the afternoon following his reading at the college. On entering my apartment he went straight to the Rouault and exclaimed, "It is almost as alive as the original! Where did you get it?" I told him about the Paris bookstore, and we talked for a good part of the afternoon about Rouault. Perhaps because of the eloquent reading Mr. Speaight had given of Eliot's *The Waste Land* the night before, the poet and the painter were joined in our discussion, since they seemed to illustrate the religious consciousness of our age better than those other figures in France born when Rouault was born, between 1870 and 1871: Proust, Valéry, Gide, Matisse, Picasso.

Both Eliot and Rouault recreate the myth of the land blighted by a curse, the land awaiting redemption by water. Life continues to survive on this land, but it has become so devoid of meaning that it is comparable to death itself. The landscapes of Rouault and his characters are caught in a strange immobility and desertion, as if they are experiencing the aridity of death much more than the fertility of life. Likewise in Eliot's poem several brief scenes serve as a mimicry of death: drinking coffee in the Hofgarten, a game of chess, a typist home at tea time. Speaight reminded me that scenes from Eliot and Rouault resemble "a heap of broken images, where the sun beats." The phrase is from Ezechiel, and Eliot uses it in the first part of *The Waste Land*.

Le vieux roi, Rouault's best-known painting of those exhibited in America, has an oriental richness and bejewelled effect which Eliot also achieves at the beginning of the second part of *The Waste Land*. With strong echoes of Shakespeare's *Antony and Cleopatra*, Eliot paints a scene of almost Byzantine ornateness. But the rich setting of Eliot's queen and Rouault's king does not deceive the artist. The meaning of life has disintegrated also, in the very midst of wealth and beauty. The old king looks inwardly at his own unresolved drama, and holds in his hand the innocence of a flower.

The London pub scene that follows Eliot's vision of a "burnished throne" serves in the same way to point out the deathlike quality of certain modes of living.

At the end of the poem, in the section called "What the thunder said," the confusion of heroes—Christ, Parsifal, the Fisher King— is reminiscent of the confusion of heroes in Rouault's paintings: a king, Christ, a clown, a judge. One thing they all have in common, these heroes of the poem and of the painting: a life which has lost its meaning, a life which is a form of death.

Commencement came a few months after Robert Speaight's visit to Bennington and to my apartment. One of the graduating seniors, Kathleen Harriman (usually called Puff), had studied with me all four years. She asked if she might bring her father, Averell Harriman, to visit me in my Old Bennington home. At that time Mr. Harriman was president of the Pacific Railroad Company. He walked into my living room and went directly to the Rouault reproduction, as Speaight had done a few weeks earlier.

"What a remarkable reproduction of *le vieux roi*! Where did you get it?"

This was said before we introduced ourselves. I was impressed that "a railroad man" recognized Rouault at a glance, but learned immediately that Mr. Harriman had purchased original paintings of the new French painters and put them in the nursery of his daughters, with the hope that the girls would grow up loving such paintings.

As he asked me to put some ice in his glass of sherry (the first time I had heard such a request), he quoted a sentence of Rouault: "Painting is only one other way of forgetting life." Since that June day in Bennington, I have tracked down the sentence: "La peinture n'est pour moi qu'un moyen comme un autre d'oublier la vie."

After Mr. Harriman finished his iced sherry, we all left to return to the college and listen to the commencement address. I did not listen too well. Thoughts about Rouault and about my two visitors who had enjoyed looking at *le vieux roi* prevented me from following the speech. The heroes of a painting, like a clown of Rouault, do not move. They represent the immobile renovation of an individual, heroes reflecting the strange, unaccountable action of thought. Unable to move from the pose in which the artist has fixed them, they are concentrating on an inner lyricism in a way characteristic of heroes of some of the greatest modern novels: those of Kafka, Joyce, Proust.

1940–1945: Trumbull College, Yale

Rouault marked the beginning of a quest for a few pictures which I wanted to have with me on my walls, as reminders of the painters who did them and of all painters who through the centuries have instinctively and skillfully drawn and painted some inner vision or model.

From my apartment in Old Bennington I moved to New Haven, to a spacious apartment in Trumbull College at Yale where I served as resident fellow. I hung the Rouault reproduction in my study-office where "King David" presided over my small collection of books. The walls of my living room were bare. My second book of criticism had just appeared, the volume following my doctoral dissertation. I called it *Clowns and Angels*, and attempted in it to study the theme of the clown in modern literature and art. In a fortuitous way that book brought me, as gifts, my next two pictures, this time two original paintings. The first came from Henry Miller who had reviewed *Clowns and Angels*. He had liked the book, whose theme was actually one of his own themes. When he visited me in Trumbull he brought with him a watercolor, inscribed to me and entitled, "The Clown's Mask." Eventually he was to send me two other watercolors, a self-portrait and a fantasy picture reminiscent of Chagall. "The Clown's Mask" was the first picture I put up in my Trumbull living room. Today one wall of my small library in Durham has all three pictures, and no others. That wall is a memorial to a man I looked upon as a friend whose words encouraged me, not only in my work, but in a desire to live and to keep such breath as I have.

One of my Yale students especially interested in French literature, Philip Walker, had come across Miller's review of *Clowns and Angels* and had asked me about the book. I had loaned him my copy. He served in the navy at the end of the war, and from the Far East he sent me as a gift a large oil painting he had done. It was the second original art work I received, the second picture I hung not far from the Miller watercolor. There was no title for Philip's work, but a note accompanied it in which he wrote, "There are too many clowns in your Trumbull apartment, and so I am sending you an angel." It was a green angel with a long face, a bald head ("angels have no hair on their bodies," Philip had written as explanation), the tip of a strong-looking wing behind his right shoulder, and two raised fingers of his right hand. He was for me immediately the angel of the Annunciation, caught at the moment when he spoke the solemn words to Mary, invisible in the painting.

A clown and an angel, related in my early book of criticism, were thus added to "King David."

1950–1962: Bingham House, Bennington College

During the 1950s when I taught both at Bennington College and at the New School in New York, my "collection" grew rapidly thanks to a varied and unpredictable series of happenings. I lived at Bennington in the faculty suite of one of the campus houses, Bingham, situated at the very edge of the campus. My living room windows looked out on small hills in the distance, which in late afternoons were often disguised by a special shade of blue which I called the blue of Tuscan hills and which in my imagination transported me to Europe. I enjoyed two worlds those years: the country landscape of Vermont, Monday to Thursday, and Manhattan, Thursday night to Sunday morning.

The change in my paltry collection came about through a new friend in New York, Henry Leffert, an English professor at City College who, each of those years in the decade, invited me to give a lecture at City College to his large class studying European literature. He opened the class meeting to nonenrolled students who might be interested, and the audience grew to a considerable size throughout those ten years.

At the end of each lecture Henry invited me to his house for refreshments and conversation, and especially for a viewing of his ever-increasing collection of modern painters. He favored the French and had on his walls at least one painting by each of the major painters, from Cézanne to Picabia. One of the talks I prepared for his class was on the friendship between Picasso and Max Jacob, and on the aesthetics of the painter and the poet-painter. That day when I visited Henry's Manhattan apartment he proudly showed me his newest acquisition, a gouache by Max Jacob. I knew about Jacob's paintings but this was the first I had seen. The subject was a circus, *le cirque Médrano*, in Paris.

Because of my talk in the afternoon, and because of my excitement in seeing the Jacob, Henry said he would ask his agent in Paris to find a Max Jacob painting for me. A month later I received in Bennington by air mail a carefully wrapped Jacob gouache, still in its ornate Paris frame. It showed the gray facade of a church in St. Benoit-sur-Loire, originally a Benedictine monastery, where Jacob had lived during the last years of his life. The signature was there in black ink. It was my first real treasure: an art work closely related to my study of French poetry. A few years later the first doctoral dissertation I directed at Duke was on Max Jacob.

On a return trip to Nice in the mid-1950s I discovered in a small art gallery close by the Negresco Hotel a Picasso lithograph of the head of Max Jacob. It was drawn originally by Picasso for a book in honor of Jacob. I explained to the owner of the gallery, a very charming and knowledgeable lady, that I owned in America a Jacob gouache. After I had purchased the lithograph, she urged me to let her keep it for a few weeks. She intended to ask Picasso, who from time to time came down from Mougins and paid visits to her gallery, to sign it. Two weeks later my copy was ready. Picasso had signed it in red pencil. The head of Jacob by Picasso now hangs beside Jacob's gouache.

My annual talks at City College continued, and thus also my visits to Henry Leffert's painting collection. On some of those visits I had to struggle against feelings of envy for such a display of beauty, but I was usually able to convert such feelings into admiration for the care and taste Henry exhibited in his choices of pictures and in the exchanges he made between those he owned and those he wanted to own. His example fostered in me the desire to increase, very modestly, my own minor collection.

On my next trip to Paris—it was another nonresident Bennington winter term—I received a letter from Henry asking me if I
would be willing to carry back with me from Paris a very small
oil painting by Renoir that his agent had bought for him. I agreed
while reminding my friend that I might encounter difficulty with
the customs officers in taking such a picture out of the country. In
his next letter Henry gave me explicit directions concerning what
to say to customs at Le Havre. The trip home was to be by boat.

The Renoir was a small painting of a girl's head. It had all the
characteristics of Renoir's art. I carried it loosely wrapped in brown
paper under my arm. At Le Havre two customs men examined my
two bags, and then one of them, pointing to the package under my
left arm, asked, "Qu'est-ce que vous portez là?"

My answer, as dictated to me in Henry's letter, was, "C'est de
l'art moderne."

This was, of course, the critical moment I had feared. With no
hesitation, and without a request to see the object, the officer said
with disgust in his voice, "Emportez-moi ça."

He was telling me to get the Renoir out of the country, and I
was thereupon overcome with a sense of guilt and with sorrow for
France, since it was losing a painting by one of its masters. I became
a successful smuggler thanks to the shrewd directions of my friend
Henry, whose Manhattan collection of French art was soon to be
enriched with the painting he had wanted above all.

He met me at the boat as we docked in New York, and stood
with me as the American customs men examined my luggage and
easily passed the Renoir painting. (They did look at it to make sure,
as they said, that it was not pornographic!) With relief and pleasure
I handed over to Henry the painting, still wrapped in brown paper.
Not until we were in his apartment where lunch had been prepared
by his sister, a French teacher in a New York high school, did he
look at the painting. The expression on his face was not that of a
satisfied art collector, but that of a man who loved beautiful paintings. All my efforts to transport a small Renoir oil and my worries
about being held up in Le Havre or New York were rewarded by
Henry's almost tearful delight.

He embraced me for the first time, and led me to a large watercolor propped up over another painting. He gave me the title: *la*

maman et l'ange. In the right-hand corner I noticed immediately a clear signature in black ink: Francis Picabia.

"This is a gift for you, to help enlarge your collection. I remember how much you admired the other Picabia I have. This *maman et l'ange*, with the hands of the mother, and the just-born baby with its red hair and green body, will shine over all your apartment. Your students, when they look at it, will learn the name of Picabia, always overshadowed in Paris by Picasso."

In recent years (not long after Henry's death), my friend Olivier Revault d'Allonnes, son of Henriette Psichari, collected the writings of Francis Picabia and published them in a handsome book. I have placed that book on a table under the painting in my living room: a graphic example of surrealist art, and the textual example of endless manifestos of the late 1920s when I first visited Paris and first heard the name of Picabia.

Very few of my students at Bennington demonstrated any real interest in the pictures that were gradually filling the spaces on my walls in Bingham House. The one exception was Miriam Hermanos, from New York. Once, as we talked about the Picabia, she said her father was a collector of French paintings. Through modesty she hesitated to talk about her father's collection. I had to question her and prod her before I realized that the paintings in her Manhattan apartment far surpassed those of Henry Leffert.

A few weeks later, one Sunday evening, Miriam appeared at my door. She was carrying a large picture covered with cloth. "This is for you, from my father. He wanted me to say that it is not very much. But he wanted you to have it."

We uncovered the picture—a lithograph by Matisse, a drawing of Saint Dominic he had drawn for the chapel in Vence that he had designed and decorated. It is a simple drawing, made up of very few lines, which Matisse had copied when he drew the huge portrait of Dominic on the back wall of his chapel. (At that time I had no way of knowing that years later, in 1978, I would offer to build a small chapel for Duke students on Campus Drive, fashioned after the Matisse chapel in Vence. My lithograph is a constant reminder of my defeat in that proposal.)

The twelve years when I lived in the Bingham House apartment were busy, crowded years for me. During the first five, 1950–55, I taught at both Bennington College and at the New School in New York. Through sheer fatigue I gave up the New School—regretfully, having enjoyed the classes there made up of students of varying ages, from eighteen to seventy, eager to study whatever I offered: surrealism, the French theater, Proust. At Bennington two courses in particular became the center of my teaching: "Theory and Form of Tragedy" and "Proust." They were years when a variety of literary commissions came to me. One of these was destined to enlarge my collection of pictures.

The New York publisher George Braziller made a suggestion that attracted me, concerning a volume of Cocteau writings. I had begun teaching Cocteau's plays and poetry in two different courses and was becoming familiar with his essays which, in comparison with his other forms of writing, seemed the most important. Mr. Braziller wanted a selection of passages from all of Cocteau's publications that would relate to his biography: his temperament, his life story, his role in contemporary music, painting, literature, theater, films, his conversations with Chaplin, Picasso, Milhaud, etc.

Eagerly I accepted this commission, began a rereading of all of Cocteau's work, and wrote to Cocteau (whom I had never met) asking for permissions and suggestions. This was the beginning of a correspondence from early 1954 to his death in 1963. During that time I met him only once, in Paris in 1960, when he looked upon me as one of his translators and took me to lunch at Le Grand Véfour.

Throughout 1955–56, since I was on leave from Bennington College, I lived in New York while teaching as a visitor at Brooklyn College and worked steadily on the translation of many Cocteau texts chosen (with or without his approval) from seven of his books. First one, then a second, and then a third drawing by Cocteau reached me through the mail, each inscribed and signed. Accompanying letters said he was having a difficult winter in Paris, where signs of hostility toward him and his work were visible and harmful. "It helps me," he wrote, "to think that on the other side of the Atlantic, you are helping me and actually working for me."

The first drawing shows two hieratic profiles facing one another from each side of the drawing. In between is the sea with a glowing sun over it. The inscription reads, "A Wallace Fowlie avec l'amitié de Jean Cocteau. 1956."

With the second drawing he had inserted a short note which urged me to preserve it carefully. He believed it might be valuable in time, since it was one of his first pictures. It shows the head of a faun, horns and pointed ears, and is entitled *Prélude à l'Après-midi d'un faune*. It was Cocteau's homage to Nijinsky, the creator of the role of the faun in Mallarmé's poem, danced to the Debussy music.

The third of these small drawings reached me soon after the second (and I wondered gratefully if Cocteau was cleaning out his stack of old drawings). This was a self-portrait done in Oxford where in 1955 Cocteau received an honorary degree (thanks to the campaign of Enid Starkie). The face in the drawing looks very much like the Cocteau I met in 1960. Above the face is Cocteau's familiar profile of an angel, which he sketched so often in his graphic work.

As the result of a curious incident in Paris I received from Cocteau as a gift a very large drawing, so large in fact that I was puzzled about how I was going to keep it with me on the plane from Paris to New York.

A few years before I did the book of translations, I spent a semester in France and Italy for the usis, giving a lecture in French on Broadway theater. The first engagement was in Paris, at the Sorbonne. At the end of that lecture (Salle Liard), a few old friends who were in the audience spoke to me. There were also a few friends of friends who introduced themselves. James Lord was one of those new friends. We had lunch the following day. He spoke of seeing Cocteau frequently and extended an invitation to me to lunch at Cocteau's house the following Sunday. I had heard of Cocteau's habit of inviting a large number of people on Sundays to whom he felt some kind of obligation. I declined the invitation without telling James that I hoped someday in the future I might have the chance to see Cocteau under quieter, more auspicious circumstances.

Monday morning I was working in my hotel room when James called to say he was bringing over a gift from Cocteau. (It was obvious that Lord had stressed, perhaps exaggeratedly, to Cocteau the fact that I had introduced his plays and novels to many American students.) Soon after the telephone call James came into my room carrying a large picture. Before removing the paper covering it, he explained what had transpired Sunday. On arriving alone he had announced I was unable to come. Thereupon Cocteau told him to go upstairs and choose from the stack of drawings one that he thought I would like. "I will sign it then, and you will take it to him tomorrow."

With those words James removed the covering and both of us examined what to me was the most elaborate and the most mythologically conceived Jean Cocteau drawing I had ever seen. A large figure of an animal, both dog and unicorn, with a human face unquestionably that of Jean Marais, was peacefully stretched out, sphinx-like. (Marais had acted in many of Cocteau's films, notably *Orphée* and *La Belle et la Bête*, and in several of his plays: *La Machine Infernale*, *L'Aigle à deux têtes*.) A bushy tail, flattened against the ground, was just above a band of words covering the lower strip of the picture. On the right, above the tail, was the sketch of a tent supported by a strong-looking pole that seemed to parallel the horn of the unicorn. To the original signature in the bottom left corner (Jean★1937), the poet had added, "à Wallace Fowlie, s'il le permet, avec mon amitié, Jean Cocteau."

The drawing was twenty years old when I received it from James Lord. He and I tried to decipher the words on the thin wavy banner over the bottom of the picture. The words we made out were clearly of an heraldic nature: *parti à l'azur à la croix patriarcale   d'or accompagne en pointe   de 3 annelets du même   à trois bandes d'or d'azur Le sire de Milly*.

Cocteau, who had purchased a house in Milly-la-Forêt, a small town outside Paris, was looking upon himself as the "Sire," the lord or mayor of the town. James and I remembered that Cocteau had often said that the poet's message is obscure, that words are omitted, that a poem, after all, is only half visible. The arcane or mythological mysteries remain in the drawing of the unicorn and in the words of the Sire de Milly. In my Durham apartment the Cocteau pictures are on the walls close to the table where I serve dinner to students and colleagues. If my cooking is especially bad

on a given evening, I can say, "Raise your eyes and feast on the
Cocteau drawings. You will not find such art in any of our best
restaurants in all of Durham County."

Across the room, on the wall beside the door of my apartment,
I have a small lithograph by Marie Laurencin (another gift from
Henry Leffert), a drawing of the heads of two young girls with
beady eyes. I placed it there to offset the head of Jean Marais as
unicorn and the angelic profiles on the other drawings of Cocteau.

My weekly trips from Bennington to New York during 1950 to
1955, when I taught two courses each year at the New School on
Thursday and Friday evenings, gave me a sense of freedom from
the more rigorous teaching schedule in Vermont from Monday
morning to Thursday noon. The "down-flier" train between Mon-
treal and Grand Central Station stopped at North Bennington at
1:30 P.M. I took it each Thursday, reached Grand Central at five,
checked into a small hotel on Madison Avenue at 38th Street, and
walked from there to 12th Street, the site of the New School. On
the way I stopped for a hamburger and coffee. My class began
at seven and ended at nine. On Friday mornings and afternoons
I relived my fascination with the city: its streets, parks, cinemas,
galleries, and crowded sidewalks.

On Madison Avenue one Friday I entered a small art gallery I had
often passed. In the window I had seen a drawing that I thought
was Picasso's. I asked about it, and the young salesgirl showed me
a large number of drawings, most of them nudes on a beach, which
she told me Picasso called "les monstres de Dinard." One attracted
me forcibly and I purchased it at a surprisingly low price. It was a
simple pencil drawing of two statuesque nude figures, girls leaning
one on the other, seated on the beach. The sea breeze was blowing
their hair. They were peaceful—hieratically so—goddesses, perhaps, impervious to human trials and sorrows. I have always placed
this drawing in the hallway in order to see it as I am leaving my
apartment to teach, or going to my bedroom to sleep. Picasso's
signature is written in the lower left corner—so lightly, discreetly
penciled that you have to search for it. I have often thought that

it is my most "valuable" picture, in terms of market value. But I would rather be reduced to ashes than sell it.

During the winter of 1954–55 (November to January) I read about a large exhibition of Rimbaud's work at the Bibliothèque Nationale. That winter I was unable to go to Paris because of my courses at the New School. The first teaching day of the spring semester at Bennington came in March. I was walking down the driveway to Bingham House, after meeting my first class, when I heard my name called out. I turned and saw Ira Hasenclever waving to me and holding up a long roll of cardboard. She taught German and French and was one of my favorite colleagues at the college.

"I have brought you something from Paris, a minor picture for your collection. It is only a poster."

Standing there in the driveway, Ira and I unrolled the Bibliothèque Nationale poster announcing the Rimbaud exhibition: it was the idealized head of Rimbaud, a detail from Fantin-Latour's large painting of Rimbaud and Verlaine and other poets in Paris. I had examined it once in the Louvre. This poster was not only decoration for my kitchen wall, it marked the beginning of my search for documents—mainly pictures—of Rimbaud, a search that was to culminate somewhat dramatically in 1966 in Nice.

Encouraged by having found a Picasso drawing in the gallery on Madison Avenue, I returned there one day in January 1955 and made two purchases. One was an etching by Jacques Villon (brother of Marcel Duchamp). It was an imaginary portrait of Rimbaud, not resembling any picture I had seen of the poet. But it incited me to start collecting, if possible, other imaginary portraits. The Fantin-Latour had been a beginning. This Villon etching was a continuation.

The other picture I purchased that day attracted me simply by the movement and the lines and the half-discernible story. It was untitled and unsigned. On the back of the picture were the words: "colored lithograph by André Masson." His name was familiar to me: a surrealist painter and the author of several brief articles on Paris art exhibits I had read in *La Nouvelle Revue Française*.

The center of the picture was filled by a handsome horse bearing a skeletonlike rider. Was he a dead rider? The sea filled the lower part of the picture with a stretched-out figure on the shore. Was that the body of the rider who seemed crushed by a large chariot wheel? A star in the right-hand upper corner seemed attached to the scene of death, and a fish hovered over the horse.

I lived with this Masson picture a year before it suddenly occurred to me that the scene might well be the death of Hippolytus —inspired perhaps by Racine's *Phèdre*. The hero had been killed by his chariot horses when a monster had emerged from the sea. Neptune had answered the prayer of the father Theseus. Much of the play's action was in the action of the picture—a surrealist view of Hippolytus.

Then in the late fifties three gifts, from very different sources, came to enrich my walls in Bingham House.

I had helped one of our first male students at Bennington, a gifted actor and play director, to secure a Fulbright Fellowship for study in Paris. He returned to the college after an exciting year observing productions of the *théâtre de l'absurde*—Beckett, Genet, Adamov, Ionesco—and presented me with a small etching (*eau forte originale*) by Manet: *portrait de Baudelaire*. This very delicate sketch of the young Baudelaire—tall hat, long hair—still remains for me a vivid memory of scenes Alan Levitt and I did at Bennington and of his lively participation in my classes.

During one of my summer visits at Yaddo, only thirty miles away from Bennington, I met Kit Barker and his wife Elsa. Kit was a painter and printmaker. He spoke often of his brother in England, the poet George Barker. When I was leaving Yaddo, he gave me as a going-away gift a print of his—the figure of a peacock with a spread-out tail. He inscribed it "to Wallace from Kit and Elsa with affection." Then to me, orally, he added, "It is in memory of Mallarmé's swan sonnet."

The third gift was the most unexpected of all. It must have been the school year of 1958–59 when I saw, almost every week, Mr. and Mrs. James Dennis, who lived in Old Bennington. Jim Dennis was a Bennington College trustee. His daughter Peggy had been one of my students during the early years of the college. The Dennises asked me to help them review their French: to read French with them and discuss in French what we read. I enjoyed those "lessons" very much. These elderly friends knew France quite well and were eager to revive their memories of geographical places, French cooking, French words and their etymologies. They examined me and I examined them, and all three of us grew to look forward to our linguistic games Wednesday evenings.

At the end of our last meeting they presented me with a picture which had been in the Dennis family for some time. It looked like an elegantly printed diploma—a *brevet* for a lieutenant's appointment in Napoleon's army. In the center is the signature: Bonaparte. At the bottom of the page is the date: *an cinquième,* the fifth year after the Revolution, and above the date a small engraving of Napoleon, made during the Italian campaign. This was not, rightly speaking, art, but it was a museum piece I was excited to receive, a document that would quite naturally find its place in my collection. I keep it on the wall of my hallway, beside the Picasso nudes.

This gift marked the end of my Bennington years. Many years had elapsed between my acquisition of the Rouault reproduction and the signature of Napoleon Bonaparte.

1966: Nice

I began my teaching at Duke University in the fall of 1964. After living my first two years in Durham in a small crowded apartment, I moved to a larger more attractive apartment in a new building: 17–D Valley Terrace. There I have lived for more than twenty years.

During the fifties and sixties I made several trips to Nice where I had found in the Hôtel Atlantic (boulevard Victor Hugo) a room suitable for the work I wanted to do in a French city, far more restful for me than Paris. In 1956 I published my translation of *The Journals of Jean Cocteau,* and in 1966 my study, *Jean Cocteau: The History of a Poet's Age.* To secure illustrations for these volumes Cocteau directed me to a professional photographer in Nice: Jean Ferrero. We became friends. Jean helped me with the pictures I needed and often drove me to places near Nice where he had work to do: Eze, Menton, Villefranche, etc. One day in late spring (I was on sabbatical leave from Duke) he introduced me to a young Nice painter: Jean Gouttin. A few days after this introduction he brought me as a gift a very small oil by Gouttin painted on a piece of wood: *Nature morte: les gobelets et carafon.* The colors are light yellow at the bottom of the picture and grow to a dark red at the top. It was for me the colors I associate with Nice, and with all of the Midi for that matter. In my guest room it is an emblem of a city I love, and a memory of my good friend Jean Ferrero.

The Swiss painter Erni is known for his illustrations of Homer, according to Ferrero, who urged me to buy a few drawings in a series of semierotic poses of a girl and boy. They were on sale in the gallery near the Negresco. Half-heartedly I purchased two. Back home in Durham I quickly tired of them, put them in my guest room, and finally gave one to my student Will Singer. I still have the other, which I keep on my wall because it reminds me of my life in Nice, of my friends there, and of my Hôtel Atlantic on the boulevard Victor Hugo.

In the summer of 1966 I worked in my room (room 428 in the Atlantic), finishing a translation of the complete works of Rimbaud. This work had been going on for two years. I was still uneasy about the exact meanings of a few words in the poems, and needed to consult a competent French Rimbaud scholar. I knew of one who lived in Nice and who had, according to all accounts, the largest collection of pictures, documents, and objects related to Rimbaud. I wrote to this man, Henri Matarasso, and told him I was finishing my translation of Rimbaud and wondered if I might have his help on a few puzzling words. He answered my note and invited me to come by on Wednesday at two.

On opening his door to me, he said, "I wish you had come yesterday. Picasso was here for lunch." (To myself I said, "Had you invited me on Tuesday, I would have come.") Matarasso led me immediately to a table in his living room. There we both bent over a drawing, obviously of Rimbaud.

When Picasso arrived the day before, Matarasso asked him if he would do a sketch of Rimbaud for his collection. Picasso consented and asked for a photograph of Rimbaud. Matarasso gave him a small copy of a photo of the poet at 16. Picasso held it in his left hand, and with his right hand sharpened his black pencil on the right side of a sheet he had tacked on a wall, and then in the space of two minutes, according to Matarasso, copied the photograph. He had changed all the details of Rimbaud's head, but copied the tie and the buttons on the boy's vest. He had lightened the face with boyish animated features and hair that stuck up from the boy's head, in today's style of punk youngsters. Picasso signed the drawing and gave it to Matarasso.

Greediness overcame me as I looked at the picture, and I asked Matarasso if he would allow me to use it for the cover of my translations. The answer was quick in coming. "Picasso was gracious to me in signing the sketch and giving it to me. I should do the same to you. I will have a copy made for you and give you permission to use it on the cover of your book." He sent me the original drawing, the last picture I added to my collection.

When the book appeared in 1966, its cover was the first commercial use of that Picasso drawing. It was a copy of that edition that the rock singer Jim Morrison wrote to me about. In a brief letter he thanked me for doing the translation of his favorite poet. That book traveled with him during the four years (1967–71) when the Doors gave their concerts. In a postscript Morrison wrote, "That Picasso drawing of Rimbaud is great."

Today there is a T-shirt for sale with the Picasso drawing of Rimbaud on it, and with the words "Go Rimbaud" printed at the top of the shirt. I am still looking for one of those Picasso-Rimbaud T-shirts, although I have ceased looking for further pictures.

PART III

Remembering Three Decades of the Young

CHAPTER 6

From the Sixties to the Seventies:
Bob Dylan, The Beatles
From the Seventies to the Eighties:
The New Myth of The Doors

What name can one use? the young? the youth of today? the late adolescents? Everything that relates to them is uncertain and changing. Ever changing. Ever uncertain. One day the features of a face and of a character will seem clear. The next day a blemish on the face and an unpredictable shadow falling over the character will give you pause: has she changed? is he different today? Today is the only moment in time for the young. The past is too close to the present to give any resonance to memory, and the future is at every minute confused with the present in order to keep it exciting and tangible.

The sixties was the decade of the young. During those years they were the center of it all. They blossomed into flower children. They lived from one love-in to another. They won every revolt and every demonstration. Just when they learned how to have sex easily, they decided that smoking pot was more necessary, and sex rites, once discovered, became secondary to being turned on each night from the grass they kept concealed in their guitar cases. The nightly trip eased all the problems and all the issues. Marijuana took over and replaced the stalwart theories on the war, justice, the establishment, methods of teaching, existentialism and structuralism, on Beckett's *Molloy* and Artaud's *Theater and its Double*.

They were exciting and infuriating, those youngsters. I believed them when they spoke in class, and outside of class, more than I believed my colleagues. They learned to read without bothering with the critics and the professors. There was only time to read the book itself, and they really read it . . . if it turned them on. The boys went for Rimbaud, and the girls for Baudelaire. They held on to those phrases that spoke to them directly—phrases that had no need of exegesis—and they used the phrases in the evenings when they sat around together drinking coffee or smoking pot. "Love has to be reinvented" was a Rimbaud phrase they clung to. "Your memory shines like a monstrance in me" was a Baudelaire line one of the girls told me she copied out at the beginning of every letter she wrote.

There came a moment in the sixties when the young stopped talking about the war. They had in a way won in their antiwar arguments and demonstrations because so many of the older generation had begun agreeing with them. Activism had become futile. The continuing war had endangered the university, the chances for future study and future jobs. They had to change their tactics just to survive: to get into a graduate school, to get work. Activism, deriving from beatism and hippieism, had had its day. The beards were being cut off or neatly trimmed. The hair was being cut shorter. There were fewer patches on the bluejeans. The kids were older. We realized this, a bit later than they did. Their blond vigor was darker.

When summer vacation came they no longer spoke of surfing and scuba diving but of construction jobs, which meant they had begun to worry about their health, about the strength and the beauty of their bodies, as well as the need to earn money and give to themselves, as well as to their fathers, the first signs of independence. There was still an element of exoticism attached to the summer jobs, but less exoticism than swimming in Mexican waters or bicycling in southern France. They began drawing up lists of serious reading for the summer, books that were referred to by their teachers, books the teachers never got around to or never dared to teach: *Finnegans Wake*, *Naked Lunch*, *The Screens*, Plotinus, Vico, Bergson.

They were critical years, especially those between 1968 and 1972, when changes took place, when the Jesus freaks briefly replaced the hippies in media attention. Suddenly the young were older. They were able to look back a few years and estimate the changes that had taken place by the phases of musical taste and singers they had successively approved.

Early in the decade Bob Dylan had been their favorite hero, poet, and singer. They had become conscious of life, of their problems of life, as they were becoming attached to "The Thin Man," "Desolation Row," and "Tombstone Blues." Bob Dylan's lessons on the hypocrisies of the older generation, on the failures of the little man, and the triumphs of the successful big man, provided them with a first indoctrination. Dylan was young, attractive, hippie-styled, a lyric rebel whose poems fused literary allusions and social awareness. Those poems had the power of a youthful spirit whose mistakes, if he made any, would be pardoned because of his charm, because of charisma.

The flat American accent of Elvis Presley and the rhythm of his gyrating hips were taken over by Dylan who, in his public performances, added allusions familiar to college students and made love to them all collectively in a voice both nasal and flat, a combination of twang and prolonged vowel sounds. A boy prophet he was, with the courage and dogmatism of older prophets who spoke in wildernesses rather than in the screaming packed auditoriums where the young of America grew together, swooned together, and lost themselves in the Dionysian ecstasy of rock rhythms.

The Beatles had filled the middle years of the decade. They continued to hold the admiration of the young until they began to split up and look older. *Sgt. Pepper's Lonely Hearts Club Band* marked the high point of their impact on the world, and especially on the young of the world. The older listeners, those thirty and above, were rejuvenated by such words and such singing. Even some of the older, so-called "classical" composers were attentive and enthusiastic. One of them, Ned Rorem, an excellent modern composer whom I met at Yaddo, told me that the songs on *Sgt. Pepper* were as fine as Schubert's. Such praise was looked upon by the young as anachronistic and meaningless.

The art of the Beatles was an education, a way of looking at the world and comprehending the world. "We hope you will enjoy the show" was the open invitation to participate. The grave on the cover of the *Sgt. Pepper* album was a symbol of reunion rather than of death. The crowd of faces on that cover showed us the early and the new Beatles—John, Paul, George, and Ringo, and all those figures who counted in the education of the young in the sixties, a fully orchestrated eclecticism. Included were Bob Dylan and Dylan Thomas, Mona Lisa and Marlon Brando, Lawrence of Arabia and Oscar Wilde, Marilyn Monroe and Edgar Allan Poe, Marlene Dietrich and Tom Mix. In the foreground the rows of marijuana plants formed a leading symbol of togetherness. Movie stars, writers, rock singers, and pot: they helped to make up the education of the young in the sixties.

The Beatles revolutionized the life-style of the young and gave us the best sounds in pop music, in rock music, in post-rock music. John Lennon, the chief lyricist, followed Bob Dylan but did not demonstrate Dylan's sullenness about life. "I'd love to turn you on," the last line in their song, "A Day in the Life," said in just a few syllables everything the songs were intended to accomplish. "To turn on" was an important phrase in the sixties, as significant as the phrase *le mal du siècle* in the 1830s and the phrase "to be committed" (*s'engager*) in the 1940s. It means more than getting high on drugs. It means so many things that it is indecipherable. It has the power to cause prejudices to disappear, to cause the ugly to appear beautiful, to turn despair into hope. It was the new synonym for love. A new meaning of love is apparent in "Lucy in the Sky," in "Lovely Rita," in "When I'm Sixty-Four," in "It's Getting Better All the Time."

By the end of the decade the Beatles were replaced by the Rolling Stones. The softness and the nostalgia of such a song as "She's Leaving Home" could not last for long. It gave over to the raunchiness of the Stones. Mick Jagger and the other four dominated the years that moved the spirit of the sixties into the spirit of the seventies.

The Rolling Stones returned to America in June 1972 and found here countless fans of approximately nine years. Elvis Presley also returned in June 1972 and gave four performances in Madison Square Garden where he found 80,000 fans, of varying ages, who had been fans for fifteen years.

When Elvis first began gyrating his hips and simulating the act of intercourse, the generation of parents aged thirty-five to forty denounced him all over the country. It was a clamor of disgust, but Elvis survived, with the primitive rock beat of "You Ain't Nothin' But a Hound Dog." He was the first of them all, the first liberator of the young, the first to set a style that was assimilated to some degree at least by all the legendary folk heroes who followed him: Bob Dylan, the Beatles, Mick Jagger, Jim Morrison, Neil Young. His twisting hips in 1972, more lithe than those of Chubby Checker, seem mild cavortings when we compare them with what is visible today on the stage and screen.

The rebelliousness of Mick Jagger was the background for a much more complex type of youth who was with us in 1973. In order to tolerate their own complexity, the young need to be mesmerized by someone. It was Mick in 1973. "Gimme Shelter," "Tumbling Dice," and "Jumpin' Jack Flash" were the new songs that initiated a new behavior in the young. It was a new period characterized by huge numbers of young people camping on big fields or hillsides, by huge gatherings where they waited for the music and also for an almost mystical feeling of togetherness. The young were together by the hundreds and the thousands. Jagger and his Stones rounded out the society of rock 'n' roll. His glittery eye makeup announced Malcolm McDowell's opening scene in *A Clockwork Orange*. His ambiguous sexuality announced the appearance of Joe d'Alessandro in Andy Warhol's *Trash*.

The age of the young that began with Elvis came to an end with Mick. But the ending continued a few years longer after it was over. The young won major points: recognition on governing boards in universities, the right to vote, sexual freedom, the position of student-trustee in some colleges.

I swear, as an older observer of their fantasies and realities, that the conscience of youth is sharper today than it has ever been, that their unwillingness to be hypocritical is deeply a part of their nature. They see through sham and convention, and associate such attitudes with the older generation: their parents, teachers, bosses, all those people who have grown fearful of life. They have reached the belief that articulated strife between the generations is useless. The young now are saying, let us have peace and silence.

Rock was a revolution that best characterizes the age I am trying to describe. It cannot be disassociated from psychedelia and social protest. The explosiveness of rock helped to form the sensibility of millions.

The life of the typical undergraduate is full: exercise and sports, dating and balling, listening to rock or folk music, flicks, bull sessions, trips, cracking the books, writing papers, writing or telephoning home, daydreaming and fantasy-making. Late adolescence or early manhood has to be a frenzied, jam-packed kind of existence because the strength and beauty of those years appear vulnerable for the first time. The fact of mortality, of death growing in every individual, is learned in those years by the accounts of war, by a scene in Shakespeare, by a poem of Baudelaire's, by the sudden incomprehensible death of a friend who had only yesterday represented the exuberance and hope of life.

The young are unable to speak of death, but they live it in the alienated forms of their culture: in films, songs, violent accidents, cosmic disasters of floods and starvation. They can shout and rant over minor infractions of dishonesty and injustice, but they remain sullenly silent about the experience of mortality.

By the 1970s and '80s the young had become temporarily the masters, those in charge, and they organized committees and meetings to give order to a new way. Then, predictably, they became burdened with the new responsibilities, and bored with the mystique of their revolution which had turned into politics. During those lengthy committee meetings which they themselves had demanded, they had glimpses of the freedom they had sacrificed. It might be better for a young man to learn rather than rule, swim in the afternoon rather than invent and impose rules of behavior. At night it might be better to make love or read Proust than to meet with trustees and deans who, even when liberal-minded, are subconsciously jealous of the young and envious of their potency, their knowing wit, their obscene language.

The remedies adopted by the young generation in the seventies —pot, rock, bisexuality, health food, the study of the psyche, gay liberation—are precisely those modes of living most feared by the generation of the fathers. Happiness for the young is chance. It is the opposite of routine. Anything that can be called routine at home, at school, in church, and in the favorite occupations of the young —sports and love—is the deadening and eventually the collapse of happiness.

That is why they make chance into a cult. The choice of a school, of a college, of a teacher, of a love partner, of a summer job, represents the practice of this chance. But the chance for happiness quickly diminishes by familiarity. So the student dreams of next term's course before the present course is half over. When he takes off from school, hitchhiking will give him the fullest experience of chance. Anything can happen in hitchhiking: disaster and ecstasy. If the experience is dull, he has only to get out at the next red light.

On a bigger scale, a visit to another country may provide the loftiest experience of chance, of happiness that can be experienced. Chance has to be anonymous and swift and easily abandoned when the slightest beginning of responsibility sets in. Whether it be an underdeveloped country—Mali, for example—or an over-sophisticated country such as Italy, the voyage is begun almost always with a close friend, a roommate, or a fellow athlete. And almost always, after a week or two, the two friends split up. The superficial disagreements are usually about means of traveling and what to look at. But the real reason for separation is to recover the maximum possibility for chance encounters, either intellectual or erotic, that the presence of a close friend would inhibit. After a few days in a new country, the dangers imagined at home diminish. The student traveler sees himself as the mythic hero looking for adventure. But he soon discovers that he has not the stature of a hero, and that the imagined adventures are tawdry when actually experienced.

For most students, traveling, by means of hitchhiking or by means of a TWA 747, is slumming or voyeurism, or a combination of both. The Place Pigalle, the via Veneto, old San Juan are the places to visit alone, after the perfunctory visits to the Louvre, the Colosseum, and the Puerto Rican beaches. But such visits, representing the epitome of chance and anonymity, are not morbid or sordid. They are the search for experiments either voyeuristic or active that will establish in the mind of the young man a set of pictures always to be remembered, against which he will establish another set of pictures representing the opposite of chance.

As if they are pages from history, my students in the eighties read about Gertrude Stein's Lost Generation of the twenties and thirties. Then they read Jack Kerouac's book *On the Road* (1957) and learn about the Beat Generation of the fifties. But that was also the glorious decade of Eliot, Frost, Auden, and Faulkner. James Dean was another figure to be remembered. *Rebel Without a Cause* was first shown in 1955. *The Wild One* with Marlon Brando had come out the year before. Kerouac had died at the end of the sixties at the age of forty-seven. In Lowell, Massachusetts, a park was named after him in 1988.

As I write these pages in the summer of 1988, I have assembled in front of me on a large desk seven or eight versions of the subject I have spoken of in many places throughout the decade of the eighties—twice in my course on French Symbolism when we came to the lessons on Rimbaud, in 1985 and 1988. This was in Old Chemistry, room 116, at Duke University. In the spring of 1986 Psi Upsilon Fraternity at Duke asked me to speak on "Rimbaud, Rock and Roll, Rebellion." We met in their commons room in Craven Quad. Then, it was in Dallas where at a meeting of the Translation Center at the University of Texas I rearranged the talk to emphasize my labor as translator of Rimbaud. I called my talk on that occasion, "Translating Rimbaud for a Rock Star."

I remember especially the evening at Furman University in South Carolina where at a dinner preceding the lecture a professor in the drama department told me he had taught Jim Morrison at UCLA. He spoke to me of a manuscript the student Morrison had done on Samuel Beckett's play *Waiting for Godot*, with its two tramps and a master-slave couple. Morrison, for his term paper, had rewritten the play in terms of the American Civil War by using Grant, Lee, and a slave! (After attending high school in Alexandria, Virginia, Morrison had studied film and theater at UCLA where he made friends with the other musicians who were destined to form his band The Doors.)

The afternoon of my day in Greenville, I spoke to about twenty-five teenagers, boys and girls who were living in a psychiatric clinic in the hospital. They had committed themselves because of various kinds of misbehavior and psychological problems. I had been asked by the doctor in charge to speak to them about Jim Morrison. All of them knew his songs and admired him. I enjoyed that hour with those youngsters and tried to answer their questions. I showed them pictures of Jim's grave in Paris. Several asked for copies of the pictures and copies of Rimbaud's poems. I had read a few of those poems in order to explain why I had become interested in Jim Morrison.

One of the boys obviously wanted to stay after the others left. When we were alone, he told me he had a large picture of Jim Morrison which covered one wall of his room at home. When I asked him how he had become attracted to Morrison, he told me he was born the day Morrison died in Paris. He was fifteen (1971–1986). Then, looking at me very steadily, he asked, "Do you know why I am here?" "No," I said, "I did not ask about any fellow or girl here."

He went on then to say that every day at home he played his favorite song, "Light My Fire." Whenever he listened to it, he felt the urge to go outside and light a fire. "Twice," he said to me, "firemen had to come to put out the fire I had started. . . . I am a young arsonist. But I know it is wrong, and the doctors here are helping me. They tell me I can get over this habit."

I was on the point of telling this boy that he had misunderstood the poem, that "fire" is really "love" or "lust." But I refrained from saying it, and did not remind him that that particular poem was written by Robby Krieger, although Jim by singing it so often had made it into his own song.

In the fall of 1987, actually on my seventy-ninth birthday, at Clemson University (South Carolina), I spoke to one of the most attentive and enthusiastic groups I had thus far met. I called my topic there, "Rimbaud and Jim Morrison: The Hero as Rebel." Again, as on other occasions, I sensed early in the talk that these college students knew the songs in the repertory of The Doors better than I did, had in fact grown up with them. I tried to explain that Rimbaud had played a similar role in my life, as inspirer, comforter, revealer. They seemed willing for me to bring in Rimbaud, and after the first few stories about this unusual relationship between two rebels—a French poet at the end of the nineteenth century, and an American rock singer—their attention easily focused on my narrative which by this time was becoming a medley of poetry, music, mythology, parental misunderstanding, filial unrest, ambition, success scorned, success hoped for.

As usual, the questions following the talk plowed into the Paris grave and the singer's death. Was Jim really dead? Wasn't he still alive? One student in a somewhat pedantic fashion kept returning to the name of the Paris cemetery, Père La Chaise. "Why is it called "Father the Chair"? In similar pedantic heaviness I gave him the origin of the name. It was named after a French Jesuit, François d'Aix de la Chaise, famous in the seventeenth century as Louis XIV's confessor. So many famous people are buried there that it is considered the most visited cemetery in Europe. Today Jim Morrison's grave attracts the largest number of visitors. On the two occasions when I visited his grave, in 1980 and 1982, the gatekeeper estimated 17,000 pilgrims came each year to pay tribute to Jim. Often fifty or more young people a day turn up: English, American, and French, especially. They bring guitars and sing quietly, reverently, as they sit as close as possible to the bust of Morrison over his grave, even if they do not believe his body is in that grave.

The Clemson student had carefully read Morrison's biography *No One Here Gets Out Alive* and wanted to know if the graves near Jim's that the singer had visited the day before his death were graves of really famous people. "I recognized a few names," he said, "Chopin and Proust, but not many others." I assured him they were all celebrities, and between us we were able to recite most of the names: the writers Balzac, Colette, and Oscar Wilde; an actress and a dancer: Sarah Bernhardt and Isadora Duncan; two composers: Chopin and Bizet; three painters: Delacroix, Ingres, and Modigliani.

The student's last question was, "Do they still have those signs between the entrance and Jim's grave, with arrows on them saying, 'Jim straight ahead'?" I reported that now the signs seem to have disappeared, but the name Jim is on several tombstones, with a small arrow pointing in the right direction. On my second visit I was told just to follow the crowd and the sound of guitars.

In May 1988, six months after my Clemson visit, I spoke to a group of high school students in Chapel Hill, just ten miles from Duke. Three hundred teenagers turned up. It was a "Humanities Festival Day," and classes were canceled. Of all my audiences thus far, this was the most joyous. Those teenagers were as attentive as the Clemson students and the middle-aged translators in Dallas, but they were more excitable. They would burst out with shouts whenever I named a song. They asked their questions from the floor, in the middle of one of my sentences, or whenever I paused for a second to catch my breath and clear my voice.

At the beginning of the talk I encouraged them to do exactly what they did: to correct my mistakes, to speak out, to let me know how much they liked Jim Morrison. With my opening remarks I said that this lyricist-singer had become a legend in their day, a myth almost, the kind of myth society was always forming. Teenagers and college students were keeping the myth alive, and for many reasons: his voice, his poems, his rebelliousness, and above all, the mysteriousness of his death.

"He is not dead," a youngster at my extreme right yelled out. "He is in Africa."

I replied, "If that is true, then he joins up with Rimbaud closer than ever. I know only one person in Paris saw him dead, the girl he was living with, Pamela. But there was a doctor's signature on the death certificate, although Jim's friends claimed Pam had forged it."

The same boy spoke again and pointed out that no doctor was found who had that name. This detail was new to me, and I thanked the boy for giving me that information. His death in Paris at the age of twenty-nine placed Morrison in the company of Rimbaud and Dylan Thomas, of James Dean and John Lennon.

At first I was puzzled by the choice of the word Doors, designating the rock group of four musicians: Ray, the pianist-organist; John, the drummer; Robby, the guitarist; Jim, the tenor-baritone singer and poet. Why The Doors? But I know now that it comes from William Blake: "If the doors of perception were cleansed,

everything would appear to man as it truly is, infinite." Aldous
Huxley took this phrase as the title for his book, *The Doors of Per-
ception.* And Jim Morrison named his band "The Doors, Open and
Closed."

Morrison said once, commenting on the title of his group and
alluding to Blake, "It's a search, an opening of one door after
another. It's a striving for metamorphosis. It's like a purification
ritual in the alchemical sense." On reading this passage, I felt the
words were probably inspired by Rimbaud as well as by Blake—
words from *Une Saison en enfer*, on poetry being the alchemy of the
word: *l'alchimie du verbe.*

At the end of the first year of The Doors' existence, a commen-
tator in *Newsweek*, announcing a concert to be held in New York,
wrote, "The swinging doors open and we will hear those eerie
songs Jim Morrison writes, as if Edgar Allan Poe had blown back
as a hippie."

Somewhat later, a very perceptive critic in *Village Voice*, Gene
Youngblood, spoke of Jim Morrison as becoming the major male
sex symbol: "James Dean is dead. Marlon Brando has a paunch.
Jim could be the biggest thing to grab the mass libido in a long
time." Then the critic moved to points closer to those I try to make
about Rimbaud. He wrote:

> The Doors' music is music of outrage. It speaks of madness that
> dwells within us all. It is more surreal than psychedelic. . . .
> Morrison is an angel; an exterminating angel.

During the writing of these memoir books when I have been searching for my own past, I have followed, often subconsciously, the examples of these two Dionysian spirits of France and America who
dared not only to open doors but also to close them. I had no idea
they would lead me into a world about which I knew very little.
These discoveries have helped me realize that a culture is trans-
ferable or translatable from country to country, from continent to
continent.

CHAPTER 7

Memory and Myth in Films

Film spectators are quiet vampires.
—Jim Morrison, *Lords of the New Creatures*

Let's reinvent the gods, all the myths of the ages.
—Jim Morrison, *American Prayer*

The words "mythology" and "myth" still call up in the minds of most of us something mysterious and godlike, stories that have many variations and that persist in reappearing disguised or half-disguised in each successive age. Ancient Greece, especially the storehouse of myths in Homer, continues to provide our modern writers with material they reexamine, reinterpret, and often entitle in such a way as to acknowledge their distant source: *Ulysses, The Infernal Machine, Equus.* Mythic heroes and heroines seem to be waiting in the wings or backstage to be called again on to the stage and to relive their story, not perhaps under the full rays of the sun but under a strong spotlight. Often in modern works we hear the ancient names themselves and watch the figures bearing those names as they appear somewhat reduced in stature, perhaps, less supernatural, less mysterious: Antigone, Electra, Phaedra, and their partners in crime or heroism—the uncle Creon, the brother Orestes, the stepson and lover of horses Hippolytus.

I have always felt that the leading characteristic of films is their hallucinatory nature. The very size of our modern screen explains this power of hallucination we may feel. The screen offers to us first a glorification of the human face, in a continuous use of close-ups, and then it offers a glorification of the whole human body. More and more, as the art of the cinema develops and as its mythology becomes more and more blatant, it glorifies the nude human body.

Made large by the lens, the human body is projected before us on the scale of the bodies of the ancient gods and demigods. When we see such images of nudity on the screen, our limited prejudiced minds think "eroticism," "degeneracy." But no, those images so magnified are there to evoke gods and goddesses, heroes and heroines of the ancient myths.

Films are sensational, far more sensational than the printed word can ever be. They have a more direct, more sensory, more emotional impact than books. In the theater the action of a play is carried on by dialogue. What we see on the stage is less important than what we hear. But in the art of the cinema the image comes first. It has been said, and I believe this to be true, that a blind man attending the performance of a play would not lose the essential part. Likewise a deaf man at the showing of a film would not lose the essential part of the work.

René Clair, in the course of his very astute comments on filmmaking, once tried to define what he considered "pure cinema." It occurs, he said, when a sensation is aroused in the viewer by purely visual means. This is why he claims that the cinema is an art dedicated to the present. We have to be present in the theater, at the present moment in our life, in order to experience a film. The film is being shown in order to fill that present moment.

I suppose that for me, when I think back on films I have watched, those that caused the greatest excitement come to mind—films that aroused fear and pity, if I use the Aristotelian terms, or those that held me by strongly erotic scenes or lavishly beautiful scenes. André Malraux used to say, "Sooner or later the dream factory falls back on its most effective means: sex and blood." The Hitchcock film is the type that inspires fear in an audience. It is a paradoxical pleasure that comes to us from this sentiment of fear caused by the reading of a book, the performance of a play, or the viewing of a film, when we are settled comfortably in an armchair at home or in a movie house and we ourselves are running no risks.

Films resemble epics of the past and seem to occupy the place in society once occupied by the epic. I suggest this despite the vast difference between visual art and literary art, and despite the pronouncement of some critics that films have nothing to do with literature. Other critics, more cautious, will say that films are an adjunct to the art of the novel or of drama, a means of photographing those forms. I have seen other views stating that film encompasses all the arts. I have even read the shocking theory that film is not an art at all, that it is merely a product for mass audiences: *Jaws*, *King Kong*.

After this rehearsal of such contradictory theories, let me reiterate my own belief that film has strong affinity with poetic art and especially the epic. It creates an illusion of life, life experienced as a series of events, and thus recalls the epic and the epic's later development in the form we call the novel. I am trying to say that film is closer to the epic than to the theater.

I prefer to use "epic" rather than "novel," because in many of its greatest instances film seems analogous to the epic and even to the epic of an early age, of a preliterate age; it is a form interpreting the power and the mystery of a myth.

A film juxtaposes images in such a way that they bring concepts to mind. Isn't this what we understand by myth?—a story whose meaning relates to a mystery, whose meaning is a concept that is totally clear to us because it reminds us of our own life. Actually the greatest mystery story for each of us is not a myth or a film but our own life. Since we are engaged in it, we don't understand it, we don't know where it is going, we don't know what will happen tomorrow or next year, or what change will take place in us a month from now. This uncertainty may explain in part our attraction to myths and films.

On every film we watch, we impinge our own life, and we see a completion to our life, a conclusion in tragedy or in happiness. This need to see a possible conclusion to the mystery and confusion of our own life was satisfied in earlier times by the reading of a novel (nineteenth century), by listening to the narrative story of an epic (twelfth century), or by watching the ritual enactment of a myth in a sunlit hemicycle theater of stone (fifth century B.C.).

I have chosen three films that best exemplify for me myth and memory. Specifically they are the films I have discussed most often with students during the past three decades. In our discussions I tried to point out what seem to me to be their mythic elements. My memory of the students in these discussions is as strong as my memory of the films. As I was often unable to convince students of my theories during those years, this is my final attempt to do so.

Fellini's Amarcord *(1974)*

The subject of Fellini's *Amarcord* is memory. It is thus announced in the title, a dialectical Roman form of the Italian verb *mi ricordo,* "I remember." Listen to the sound of the word: *amarcord, cord, accord—* that is, agreement, harmony. The meanings proliferate immediately as the pictures, the many sequences, review the past of a man's life to lend some sense to his present, and to the present life of all those who view his film. It is a long film, as all epics are long, and no one spectator will find all the parts equally meaningful or equally successful. The duller parts of the film—and they are not the same dull parts for everyone—are there for the viewer's rest, to prepare and highlight the more exciting parts.

All art is autobiographical. *Amarcord* is a consolidation of memories: a year in the boyhood of Fellini, from one spring to another in his birthplace, the seaside city of Rimini in the late 1930s. There is no clearly developed central character, although the boy Titta is the surrogate of director Fellini, and there are no firmly established boundaries of sequences or scenes. The film is memory, and therefore it is reality changed by distance and imagination.

Everything in the film is recognizable to Federico Fellini, of course, but also to us, and yet nothing is absolutely real. We identify, no matter what our sex or age or nationality, with the sixteen-year-old Titta, and we recognize, although we may never have been there, the streets and squares and tobacco shops of Rimini. Momentarily these streets replace streets from our personal memory. This is part of filmic hallucination.

In speaking once about all of his films, Fellini said that with every movie he revisits his life as a fantasy of the past. In *Amarcord* he revisits fascism in a small town where thugs try to force Titta's father to disavow his belief in socialism. We see the boy's early encounter with sex, where buttocks and breasts appear overwhelming to him.

The boy's father is enraged when his son urinates on a bishop's hat from a movie house balcony. At one moment in time a transatlantic liner passes close to the shore and attracts the excited gaze of the town's citizens.

In *Amarcord* a single protagonist is replaced by Fellini's imagination during the experience of remembering. This gives the film an autobiographical form. At the beginning we see the floating fluff balls, called, I believe, *le manine,* that herald the coming of spring. Then to mark the end of winter we watch the bonfire and the ritual burning of a witch (a rag doll).

Such poetic visions rising up from the subconscious alternate with realistic scenes: activities of politicians, pedants, aesthetes, earth mothers, priests hearing confessions. When a radiant peacock lands on the town fountain in an immaculate snowscape and spreads its tail, we feel that such a scene is related to our own dreams. When Titta's grandfather is lost in the fog and believes he is dead, spectators may be reminded of the atmosphere of nightmares.

We watch in *Amarcord* a profusion of memories. In this film of 1974, Fellini's boyhood is memorialized. It is a series of anecdotes, but it is so shaped that it appears to be all of one piece. It is comic and sad as it depicts small-town bravery and small-town braggadocio Italian-style.

This type of film may not recall one specific myth because it is an entire mythical world, the source of myths. Monsters and gods are called up in Fellini's imagination in all of his films, because for him all reality is legendary. No one man can be accurately defined. We can never be sure of a man's actions, of his speech, of his desires, of his sensations, of his ambitions. That is why Fellini's world is uncertain and fantasy-ridden. He is simultaneously a social historian and a poet. Titta is both attracted to the monsters around him and repulsed by them: prostitutes, goddesses, ecclesiastics, parasites, artists, assassins. *Amarcord* was made by Fellini when he was sixteen and when he was fifty-seven.

I happened to be in Rome the winter (1971–72) when Fellini was casting and shooting his film on Rome, to be called *Roma.* Every morning I would read in the newspaper *Il Messagero* the list of types

Fellini wanted to interview that day. He would give their height, weight, color, age, and a few unusual traits he hoped to find. I eagerly examined those descriptions each morning, hoping I would qualify and might try out. In one of the lists I read, "type of teacher (*professore*), seven feet tall, with features of an alligator (*alligatore*)." I sensed that was the closest I would ever come, and presented myself that morning for examination at the Cine-città. Fellini did not examine me, but one of his assistants did. I was turned down: "You have the look of a *professore* but you do not look enough like an *alligatore*." I was disappointed, but happy too, because at a distance across the huge studio I saw Fellini sitting Jove-like in a big chair and turning down, one after the other, thirty to forty flashy Roman youths, as anxious as I was to be in his film.

Kubrick's Clockwork Orange *(1971)*

A Clockwork Orange was first shown in 1971. Stanley Kubrick, an American director who works in England, based his film on the novel by Anthony Burgess and cast Malcolm McDowell in the role of Alex. Behind Alex, as he is played by McDowell with his own particular talents—athletic, facial, vocal—one could see many ancestors: the Byronic dandy from England, the decadent aesthete Des Esseintes from France, *l'homme révolté* from Camus, and *l'homme engagé* from French existentialism. If we move back farther in time, much farther, we could see diabolical traits, those of Lucifer the archangel who originally was pure in heart, as Alex doubtless had been, but who was attracted to rebellion, to all variations of sexual experience, to all experiments with decadent taste.

Young artists today vituperate against the establishment, as young artists of the nineteenth century talked against the bourgeois spirit. Bourgeoisie and establishment are synonyms, and they call to mind such concepts as security, the home, success, health. But these are not great spiritual goals. Alex is the heroic figure waging war on the bourgeoisie. He is the teenager who has gone beyond rock, back to Purcell and Beethoven. For his masturbatory fantasies he listens to Bach, Mozart, and Ludwig van's Ninth. He may appear despicable and terrifying in certain scenes, but he has the grace of wit and energy and imagination that is probably demonic. Behind Alex is the primal myth of Cain, man as the remorseless killer.

The pathological traits of Alex come from his devotion to rape, ultraviolence, and Beethoven. Alex appeals to what is dark and primal in all of us. The plot of *Clockwork* comes more from mythology than from fiction. Alex is the hero of our subconscious and dream world, caught between the sweet orange of the round world of humanity and the infernal clockwork of technology that may explode at any moment.

During the first part of the film we watch what Alex does to individuals, and then we watch what society does to Alex. The Ludovico treatment scientifically rehabilitates Alex and he is transformed quite literally into a bootlicker. By then we realize that what Alex does to others is far less horrible than what society does to Alex. At the end he is restored to his role of agile rebel. The fear of science altering human personality is a common mythic nightmare of the twentieth century.

Rimbaud's Desert as Seen by Pasolini *(*Teorema, 1968*)*

Earlier than *Amarcord*, earlier than *A Clockwork Orange*, I was able to see in Nice Pier Paolo Pasolini's film *Teorema*. The year was 1968, when I had published my translation of Rimbaud, and when Jim Morrison was reading Rimbaud and reflecting him in some of his own lyrics. Throughout *Teorema* the influence of Rimbaud is so apparent that as I watched the film—three times—I felt I was reliving almost line by line my study of the French poet.

Pasolini was both author and director of his film. The title "theorem" is justified in the rigorous working out of a problem which the film reveals. It is a term used mathematically as well as mystically. The full title might well be given as "The theorem according to Pasolini," to complement the title of his earlier film, *The Gospel According to St. Matthew*. *Oedipus*, another Pasolini film, is the supreme example of a mathematical demonstration of fate as the machine of the gods that explodes at a given moment and annihilates the protagonist-hero.

As the triangle was used in the Middle Ages to designate the mystery of the Trinity, so the theorem was used by sixteenth-century French poets to represent the mystery of the Redemption. *Théorèmes sur le sacré mystère de notre rédemption* by Jean de la Ceppède, for example.

Teorema is a vision presented in the form of a demonstration. It starts with the image of a handsome young visitor reading Rimbaud; vibrations extend from him that touch and alter each member of a wealthy Milanese family. At first only the cover of the book is visible, but those spectators who know the iconography of Rimbaud recognize the sketch by the poet's friend Ernest Delahaye: Rimbaud with his hair combed back "in the style of Parnassian poets." Later in the film the Visitor reads out loud to two members of the family the last few lines of Rimbaud's text, *Les déserts de l'amour*. By this time in the film the two key themes have been lucidly established as the desert and love.

There are two derivations here: the spiritual meaning of Rimbaud's desert of love, and a familiar plot in erotic literature, in which a young man, either a visitor to a family or a member of the family, seduces in one scene after another every member of the family, including servants. This is the plot of Guillaume Apollinaire's pornographic story *Les Exploits d'un jeune Don Juan*, and it is the general plot of *Teorema*. The accusation of pornography was made of Pasolini, although the film's meaning and its beauty make it into a contemporary work of mysticism, drawing upon sexuality, the desert of Exodus, Jeremiah, and the prose poems of Rimbaud.

Who is this intruder, whom we will call the Visitor? His arrival is announced by a telegram, and his departure is announced by another telegram when the family is seated around the dining room table. Much of the film transpires between the two telegrams, which are mysterious signs, or commands, coming from the outside. The English actor Terence Stamp, who plays the Visitor, is quite literally a foreigner to this Italian family. He speaks very little. The few Italian words he utters may be dubbed. He is the "guest" whose origin is never made clear, although his function is closely related to that of redeemer, of doctor, of a divine emissary who will bring about a cure or at least a change in the lives of those he encounters.

One thinks of Eliot's *Cocktail Party* and the doctor, both psycho-analyst and miracle worker, who first mingled with the guests and later interviewed each one separately. In the same way we see the Visitor in *Teorema* first in a gathering of young people, students from the *liceo,* relaxing after school. He is casually introduced to the family. A girl asks the daughter of the family, "Who is that boy?" (Terence Stamp looks more Nordic than Latin.) She asked the question in English, and the answer in English is, "A boy." The meaning of *Teorema* depends on what interpretation is given to the role of the Visitor. He bears no specific name.

The first member of the family to emerge with any degree of clarity is the young son Pietro, aged seventeen or eighteen, a charming, gracious fellow, affable and at ease with others. He is an athlete and has an easygoing relationship with his family. His real interest is painting. At the end of the film he has left his family to work alone in a studio where he appears to be seriously disturbed as he goes about painting. We see him pouring paint from a can on to a canvas, and we see him urinating on to a blue canvas placed on the floor. Pietro is a redhead, bearing a strong resemblance to van Gogh. The resemblance is all the more marked in his final scene of madness.

The Visitor's first important scene is with Pietro. It follows the social scene when the two fellows enter Pietro's bedroom, where there are two beds. As they get into bed there is almost no conversation. The scene depicts the growing tension in Pietro and the balanced naturalness in the older boy. The son is handsome in a boyish way, and the Visitor is beautiful as an angel ought to be. The expression on his face is always angelic, as it had been in Stamp's earlier role as Billy Budd.

In only one scene does Pietro speak at any length with the Visitor —just after the Visitor's departure is announced. He speaks then, not in the language of his age, but in a serious philosophical language, saying "You have revealed to me the self I have tried to hide. I tried to believe the daily self, the social-athletic self was real. Now I know it isn't. What is to become of me?"

The maid in the family, the shy peasant girl Emilia, played by Laura Betti, is more moved by the presence of the Visitor than all the others. Twice we see her receive and sign for a telegram, the first one announcing the Visitor's arrival, the second calling him away. The young lad delivering the telegrams dances about between the entrance to the estate and the door, a caper that is half demonic, half angelic. He teases Emilia, pleads for a kiss, but she is impervious to his charms. In the first instance she is waiting for the revelation, and in the second she has seen it: the Visitor representing felicity.

Emilia's first big scene is on the lawn. Pasolini uses the vast lawn as a graphic means of showing the tragic distance between human beings. Invisible lines stretch out between the estranged figures —Emilia and the Visitor at first—to form the design of a theorem. The lawn spreads out like the desert that is shown after each sequence. The desert is the classical symbol of dryness and repentance; its use culminates in the final episode where, for the first time, one of the characters (the father) is seen walking over it. The lawn and the desert are the same endless space where two human beings cannot meet.

Emilia is raking leaves on the lawn, and, at some distance from her, the Visitor sits reading a book, his legs spread far apart. Emilia is looking not at the Visitor's face, but at his body. When her longing for the boy reaches a peak, she runs across the lawn into the kitchen and attempts to kill herself with gas. The Visitor follows her and interrupts the suicide attempt. He drags Emilia to her room, stretches her out on her bed, and then, as if to pacify and cure her, lies on her as the prelude to intercourse.

When the Visitor leaves the house—this is a culminating moment in the life of each character—Emilia becomes a saint. She returns to her farm, refuses to eat anything except boiled nettles, heals a sick child, is seen suspended in the sky, and at the end is covered with the dirt of a ditch. Only her eyes are left uncovered. Thanks to the seduction-cure of the Visitor, she enters into another kind of life.

The wife, Lucia, is played by Silvana Mangano. Until the arrival of the Visitor she had been bored with her existence as the beautifully dressed wife of a wealthy man. Like Emilia she is sexually aroused by the physical proximity of the Visitor. One morning (the children are at school and her husband is at the factory) she hears the Visitor racing with a dog through a wooded swamp close to the house. She takes off her clothes and throws them from the porch to the ground, a floor below. She stretches out naked on the porch and waits for the stranger. He comes, with the dog at his side, and calls out, "Lucia." "*Sono qui,*" Lucia answers. When he looks at Lucia, he shows little surprise, as if he had controlled the scene. Again his smile is a combination of innocence and ambiguousness. He makes love to her in a totally simple, chaste way, because love is a sacrament in this film.

Paolo, the father, is ill, and his daughter Odetta watches the Visitor attempting to cure him. In one scene the convalescent is in a chair on the lawn, attentive to the Visitor, who is reading Rimbaud. This time he reads out loud. Odetta photographs both men, but concentrates on the Visitor who assumes comic poses and sexual poses in which he exhibits himself.

Paolo is the figure in the film who has gone deepest into the desert, deepest into the desolation of himself. The opening sequence shows the desert of the factory, a vast uninhabited expanse seen at the end of the day when the workers have left. After the desert-like factory scene, we see Paolo in the desert of his king-sized bed where, close to Lucia, he cannot consummate the sexual act. At the end of the film, in a railroad station scene, Paolo undresses and begins to walk off. The camera then moves to the desert where at a great distance Paolo appears, naked, half walking and half running with difficulty because of the sand and the wind and his exhaustion. He is naked to his fate. A piercing cry from Paolo ends the film. It is a Saint-John-the-Baptist cry in the desert where there is no one to hear him.

The love—momentary as it is—that the Visitor shows for the three women and two men is the action of the film. Each of the five characters looks to the Visitor for sexual fulfillment and receives it. Thus each of the five lives is momentarily removed from the desert, but each finally returns to the desert after the departure of the Visitor.

The film is the work of the poet-cinematographer Pasolini. Rimbaud's prose poem *Les déserts de l'amour* provides a clue to *Teorema*. The text is studied silently by the Visitor as he reads to himself, and in one scene with Odetta and Paolo, he reads out loud a few sentences from the end of the poem. They are two sentences about the visitation of a being or angel who entered the daily life of the poet, manifested kindness, and then left forever.

Each of the major scenes is a confession; the Visitor is the priest listening to the confession. The sexual act he performs with each is the absolution. The role of Terence Stamp is comparable to those of Oedipus and Jesus in Pasolini's two earlier films. The supernatural Visitor comes in order to break down the sterility of the men and women he visits. The offer he makes of his sex is both natural and sacred.

In Exodus the Chosen People reach the Promised Land by way of the desert. The prophet Jeremiah speaks of God's love for Israel, and Israel's love for God. Midway in the film the narrator recites a short passage from Jeremiah (20:7) about the derision the lover feels in others: "Everyone mocketh me." At the end of the film, naked Paolo crosses the desert as if he were following the column of fire.

Rimbaud himself seems to be speaking in *Les déserts de l'amour*. In several passages the poet could be the boy reading in *Teorema*, the mysterious Guest (as in Eliot's *Cocktail Party*) who sees in retrospect what the film is revealing:

> It's a woman I saw in the City. . . . I saw her in my bed, completely mine. . . . It was the family house. . . . She, a worldly woman, was offering herself. . . . I went into the endless city. O weariness! . . . Finally I went to a place full of dust.

As in *Teorema*, Rimbaud's dream is a series of hallucinations, mingling rustic and urban scenes that transcribe a great spiritual effort. There is more sadness than anguish in *Teorema*, and this is also true of Rimbaud's prose poem. The *Théorèmes* of Jean de la Ceppède contain the sum of Christian doctrine. Like them, the sequences in *Teorema* are pictures, highly colored and concrete, each one depicting a change from the boredom of routine to a physical adventure that propels each character into a desert where spiritual fulfillment may be reached.

CHAPTER 8

Students and Teachers: The Restless Dialogue

Oh tell me where your freedom lies
—Jim Morrison, *The Crystal Ship* 1967

From the days of Socrates through the centuries there has circulated the tradition saying: the great teacher does not write, he speaks. Thus he is free to say many things that can never be remembered exactly, that can never be used for or against him. If the lesson is not a written text, the teacher is free to instruct, inspire, shock, amuse, and even contradict himself. The teacher is free to use whatever tone he wishes, and as many tones as he wishes: sarcastic, lyric, polemical, ecumenical.

Teaching includes everything. The threat of dispersal and dilution is ever-present in the classroom, and instinctively the student knows when to open his notebook. That means for the moment that his mind is closed and that he is copying down matters that will count in some practical way. He has come into the classroom partly for this organization and reorganization of subject material. He knows when the introduction to the class lesson is casual. He knows that the promises made by the teacher at the beginning of the hour are promises that may never be kept. He knows there will be considerable talk around the subject—gossip, entertaining talk not to be consigned to a notebook. When the real subject is reached, the time is up, or almost up, and the promises will be repeated for the next class.

There is nothing that cannot be used in teaching—reason for rejoicing and dismay. The art of improvisation is the subtlest and the most difficult part of both acting and teaching. The points I hope to make in a class are usually fixed in my mind before I go into the room. But the state in which I come to class is best translated by *angst*. I pray at that moment for guidance and influx because the articulation of those points is influenced by many things: a casual question, a joke about headlines in the morning paper, mention of a film seen the night before. Even such matters as these may be put to work economically and help to bring out some meaning.

When a class begins, I am almost always guided by a single motive or a single motif. But after five minutes, I find it difficult to act from such singularity. I begin wondering whether the boundaries of a course should be delicate and evasive. From my own past I remember the sullen irritation that would overcome me when the teacher never quieted down enough to address himself to the alleged subject.

All institutions are changing, the university more slowly than others, far more slowly, for example, than the church. Traditionally the university stood as the great disciplinary power for the training of the young. The young looked at the university with some degree of awe and fear. And the university looked at the young with suspicion and some degree of hostility.

This cleavage between the institution and the student was emphasized for me some years ago in a letter from Henry Miller (written after he had spent two weeks with me at Yale). He wondered how a professor at Yale could be interested in his (Miller's) work. And if he was interested in such books, how could he stay on at the university? Miller wanted all universities to be destroyed. He called them "penal institutions of the mind."

Students are beginning to test their teachers with their frankness, their opinions, their language—even as a "tough" writer will test his readers and see how far he can go in violent action, slang, and obscenity: Miller, Mailer, Burroughs, for example.

The ideal class in literature considers intently a given text of sufficient power and beauty and mysteriousness. The students are eager to understand the meaning of the text and the reasons for proclaiming its importance. They can be held by the resources of such an exegesis: the use of allusions in the text, the appropriateness of metaphors, the rhythm of the words and their possible relationship to the meaning of the passage, the role the passage plays in the work as a whole.

Such a study represents the ultimate concentration in classwork, and the most rewarding. But if it is the exclusive class exercise, if all related biography, history, and even philosophy is banished, there is a real danger of wearing the students out and of irritating them. Close textual scrutiny is the most exciting part of any literary course, but it has to be prepared so that the appetite will be aroused. There has to be something like a background for such scrutiny.

I feel it is wrong to scorn giving such background; in that way a literature course, before it becomes an exegesis, is a means of relating the career of a writer and the accomplishments of his art to history, philosophy, psychology, and anthropology, as well as to the dreams and ideals of the students themselves. The purely exegetical part of the course will mean the most to literature specialists, to the future writer and the future teacher of literature. But even they will have to learn something about how to hold and stimulate the premedical, prelaw, preforestry student.

The student coming from science or political science or from some other very affirmative, very positive study into a literature course may well be disturbed or irritated when straight answers to everything are not forthcoming. A student in a course I was giving recently on the modern theater raised in a rather violent way questions about violence in the new films. I did not know any truthful answer to his questions and tried to tell him why I couldn't or wouldn't formulate specific answers. After class, in a state that was close to anger, he came up to my desk, threw his books on it, and shouted, "Aren't you supposed to be a critic or something, and give us answers to our questions?"

I tried in vain to point out to this student, who was specializing in history, that if I pretended to answer his questions I would be not a critic but a soothsayer.

Students have no more questions and no more answers than I do. But they have more need. They are desperately anxious to learn how to live, and when they look at me quizzically as I try to explicate a difficult poem by Mallarmé, I often feel inclined to break through the analysis and say to them, in the words of Kenneth Burke, "After all, literature is the equipment for living." Then, if I began to speak in my own words, I would say that literature today, as well as theology, has to relate and can relate its language, symbols, and insights to our experience. When Allen Ginsberg chants his poem-prayers, life is being celebrated.

If I could teach students that the survival of form in a sonnet by Petrarch, by Ronsard, by Milton is the surfacing of layers of culture for their enjoyment, then I believe I could convince them that one can come to the end of alienation and inner solitude.

Sixty years ago Abbé Morel lectured to the students at the Sorbonne on Picasso. During the course of the lecture he showed slides of several works by Picasso which were at that time the newest and boldest. The students, unaccustomed to such forms, howled and whistled and jeered at each picture. Then, without transition and without explanation, the priest showed slides of Romanesque sculpturing, statues in twelfth-century churches in southern France. The trick worked perfectly. The students, believing the works to be Picasso's, continued to hoot and stamp their feet. When Abbé Morel explained what he had done, in shifting from Picasso to twelfth-century art, the students, after a moment of surprise, began deriding themselves and applauding the mystifier. Their juvenile honesty was admirable.

Today's student does not feel as captive as he used to feel a few years ago. He is not constrained, not timorous. He is watchful, he is curious, and he is attentive when he feels the lesson has been well prepared by the teacher and related directly or indirectly to his major preoccupations. These goals, I would say, have not changed throughout the years: discovering the world, choosing a vocation, analyzing the problems of love and sports, and wondering how he can write that paper that is due and be happy tonight and tomorrow night.

He still lacks knowledge, yet he is aware of what is going on around him and what is going on in almost every country of the world. He knows something about the newest developments in art and literature, in politics and music, in philosophy and science. And that is infinitely more than I was aware of at the age of eighteen.

It is difficult for older generations to realize this new power of awareness in students today, their acquaintance, even if superficial, with so many subjects; their discussions, even if naive and repetitious, of so many problems, ranging from Zen Buddhism to pop art, from nuclear warfare to the sharp critical statements of Mick Jagger and Rod Stewart, from racism and sexism to the theater of the absurd.

On the whole the American teacher is sensitive to the needs and the power of students. I would say woe to the young person entering upon such a vocation without realizing this new understanding of students. The criticism of undergraduates is milder than that of graduate students. I listened the other day to a graduate student at Duke (not in my own department) complaining about everything: courses, requirements, the university, Durham. . . . Finally I pointed out to him that if Aristotle and St. Thomas were giving those courses at Duke, graduate students would still be indignant about bad teaching and the teacher's lack of knowledge. I have come to believe that graduate students should expect nothing. They should just be surprised if anything fairly good comes their way.

It is foolhardy and even immoral to hope to be impersonal and objective in the classroom. After the formal pattern of the teaching is done, and even while it is being done—the study of the genre of the work, the analysis of the poem's prosody, the principal agon of the play, the possible sources of the novel's protagonist, and all the other aspects of literary study that are brought out in the classroom —after all that and during all that, there is the teacher's obligation to bear testimonial to what he is teaching.

But what kind of testimonial? Moral? Aesthetic? Archetypal? Anthropological? Testimonial, I would say, to all of these. The teacher is inevitably the man who exposes his feelings to students who are ten or twenty or thirty years younger than himself. To take sides with such a writer as D. H. Lawrence or James Joyce is a spiritual striptease for a teacher. If in expounding the writings of Gide (*Les Faux-Monnayeurs*, for example), the teacher emphasizes the boredom and the corruption of respectability Gide speaks of, and the need to safeguard man's freedom or *disponibilité* before all experiences, he opens himself to criticism of a moral order.

Within the space of a generation our attitude toward the literary hero has changed, because our attitude toward man has changed. The tragic hero was once canonized by artists and critics and moralists as a human figure in defeat, as a man crushed and humiliated by a force or a fate he was unable to avoid. Oedipus, Antigone, Hamlet, and Phèdre were elevated in their degradation and set apart from ordinary men and women by their simple powerful designation as "tragic" figures.

Even the word "tragedy" now seems pompous and false. The terrors and mysteries of the modern hero are not those of Electra or Prometheus or even Hamlet. We tend to call him today the antihero because the energies he finds in himself are primal and nonethical. In the classical sense, tragedy is a man (Oedipus) or a woman (Antigone) in conflict with the moral code of their city. Each suffers because of the city's law.

The modern hero is indifferent to the city's law because he judges it basically false and arbitrary. There is a law more just than the city's; it is the law of his body, of his conscience, of the deepest, most primitive part of his human nature. Tragedy in the classical sense has no meaning for the outsider, the pariah, the rebel, the hippie, the profligate, the midnight cowboy, the easy rider.

During the past ten years the question asked me most often by students is, what is a critic? What is the difference between a critic and a scholar? When pushed to the wall for a brief answer, I usually say that critics are professional interpreters of genius. Scholars work especially from an historical perspective and thus run the risk of losing contact with the living literature of their day. As students become increasingly aware of what a critic is trying to do, they tend to place him among those types of critic who represent a very specific method of criticism: the Freudian critic or the Marxist critic or the folklorist or the semiotician.

Isn't the role of the critic the establishment of some kind of agreement or rapport between the writer and the public, between the writer and a literature class in a university? The theater, more than other literary arts, depends on a public. At the rare moments when new plays have been supported by a public—French classical theater in the age of Louis XIV, and the theater of the absurd in our own day—the public was largely composed of connoisseurs, critics themselves: the public at Versailles attending first performances of Molière and Racine, and university audiences in America attending and applauding performances of Ionesco and Beckett and Albee.

Literary quarrels are usually quarrels between present-day literature—its programs and ambitions—and literature of the past—its achievements and longevity. Here, as can be expected, students are almost inevitably on the side of the present. And here the cleavage between professors and students is visible and at times painful. Professors tend to develop a vested interest in the past and a morbid fear of the future. On one occasion Harry Levin compared professors to the slaves of some deceased pharaoh who remain in the tomb with their dead master. Such an attitude is not unrelated to the dreariness of so many of our doctoral dissertations, where work is too often done for the sake of doing work that when completed seems laborious and irresponsible. Research should be adventurous and the product of constructive and imaginative minds.

On all sides, perhaps particularly in French literature courses, our students hear the cry constantly reiterated that the twentieth century (its latter half) is primarily a century of criticism. Schools of criticism have proliferated: psychoanalytic criticism as provided by Marie Bonaparte in her long study of Poe; the Marxist criticism that flourished in the thirties and forties; and today the complex school of criticism referred to as structuralism and deconstruction.

Each of the new major critics demonstrates his own emphases, his own obsessions—like any other writer. Each critic seems fascinated by one image or concept which he exploits from volume to volume of his essays. It is the "circle" for Poulet; the Oedipus complex for Mauron; the eye for Starobinski; sadomasochism for Sartre; childhood traumatism for Weber. A great deal is demanded of students if they read these critics. Their culture will have to approach the culture of the critic they are reading if they hope to read him with maximum intelligence. Because of the disparity between the student's culture and the critic's culture the student is easily defeated by a sense of hopelessness. What holds him the most is the effort of the critic to explain the inexplicable—namely, genius.

Everything in our world today points to the end of an era and to the beginnings—the tentative, perhaps faltering beginnings—of a new era when the patterns and ideals will be set by the young, when the world will be refashioned by the very special lucidity and recklessness and fearlessness of the young. Those under thirty, I am almost willing to say those under twenty, know today that everything has to be reinvented. This is a verb (*réinventer*) associated with that adolescent poet Arthur Rimbaud.

By "everything," I mean literally that: love, marriage, sexuality, the reality of man and the incessant dialogue he carries on with himself about that reality, about his solitude, his fury, the various forms of mysticism that tempt him.

In the Middle Ages and the Renaissance the artist tried to reconcile man with God. In the neoclassical age and the Enlightenment writers tried to reconcile man with his powers of reason. In the nineteenth century man had to be reconciled with science. In the twentieth century the major artists have attempted to reconcile man with both his conscious and subconscious self. This effort is visible in the works of such different writers as Proust and Joyce, Saint-John Perse and Beckett.

No one text has ever totally represented its age, but there are scattered examples of texts representing a great deal of their age, if not all the complexities of the age. If I had to teach the Middle Ages, with only one text at hand, I would choose Villon's poem in which he imagines his mother reciting, as a *ballade* to Our Lady, *Dame du ciel, régente terrienne*. The spirit of the Renaissance is in *Hamlet*, and the classical ideals are in *Phèdre*. But after that, after the age of Louis XIV, it becomes more difficult to choose one text by which to explain the Enlightenment, romanticism, realism, symbolism, surrealism, existentialism, structuralism. For all of these more modern movements, no single text seems adequate—until perhaps we reach the last decade or two, when matters political and aesthetic have become paradoxically both more turbulent and more clear. The fury of man today was first transcribed in such theatrical works as Peter Weiss's *Marat/Sade*, the plays of Brecht, and Jean Genet's *The Blacks* and *The Screens*. The mimed terror in these plays is reenacted in our wars, our strikes, our student rebellions, our race riots, and our acts of terrorism.

If here again I had to limit myself to one text, I would choose *Waiting for Godot*, which was first performed in the 1950s, but which has grown into itself during the sixties and seventies; until now it seems, even to those students reading or seeing it performed for the first time in the eighties, the representative text of our dilemmas.

When it was first performed in Paris in January 1953 in the tiny Théâtre de Babylone, it was immediately considered a *succès de scandale,* almost an outrage, at least a hoax. Nothing really happens during the course of the play. Two men wait during two acts for Godot, who never comes. And yet this Beckett play presented a haunting image of the human situation. It compelled the audience, even those people who attacked it, to think for themselves. *Godot* has become for us today an open text, obvious in its general meaning, fairly easy to analyze in terms of the effect its performance has on an audience. *Godot* is now part of our mythology.

Originally, by all the first critics, it was called a play on the theme of man's hopelessness. But it is more and more clear today that *Godot* does not testify to man's hopelessness. There are five characters: the two tramps Vladimir and Estragon; the strange couple of Pozzo and Lucky, the master and slave in the first act, who reverse their roles in the second act; and the young boy who appears briefly in each act to tell the tramps that Monsieur Godot will not come today but that he will come tomorrow.

In the relationships they form with one another, these five characters tell us more about ourselves than they tell us about themselves. By the end of the second act, a fairly close repetition of the first act, we realize that it is not hopeless to confront reality. The two tramps have an awareness of their situation which is the situation of man. They incarnate, in both a theatrical and a philosophical sense, the little man, the Chaplinesque tramp, or Henri Michaux's indestructible Plume. Woody Allen is a recent variation on this type, and Woody Allen has certainly the ambition to represent all men.

The Beckett tramps have the courage to face the worst about

man, the worst about human nature. They assert their existence in the dark, on the edge of existence, where there is almost nothing to go on, and the courage they show in this assertion is not unlike the courage that Oedipus shows in confronting his guilt.

The Actors Workshop of San Francisco played *Godot* to an audience of 1,400 convicts in San Quentin penitentiary where the central action of the play—waiting—was more poignantly felt than by most audiences. Martin Esslin reported what one of the prisoners said, and it is worthy of counting among other interpretations: "Godot is society. He's on the outside." One of the teachers in the prison added a further commentary when he said that the prisoners knew instinctively that if Godot did come, he would only be a disappointment.

Immediate reactions to the play vary from country to country, from theater to theater, and from year to year. It is played to the most sophisticated theatergoing publics in the capitals of the world, to university students and teachers of every nationality, to general audiences in the provinces. Such different audiences relate the play to their own lives first, and then, in the perspective of a little time, begin to realize that Vladimir and Estragon wait . . . and they see that waiting gives them strength to live on. The critics too wait . . . in order to reconsider their first considerations. Eric Bentley and Norman Mailer have both returned to their initial criticisms and altered them.

In trying to teach in class several texts by Samuel Beckett, I have felt that what Beckett has learned from living (and from reading Dante) coincides with a temperament that is in my students more than in me. This may be the clue to Beckett's growing and continuing success. Adamov, Genet, Ionesco are already relegated to the past of the theater, whereas Beckett is still in the avant-garde.

Throughout my years of teaching, one kind of student has been the most difficult to help and to satisfy. He or she is the gifted young writer who chafes under the strictures of the classroom, under the assignment of papers to write and examinations to prepare, who believes he does not want to be a critic, and who is certain he wants to be a creative writer, a poet, a novelist. When this student does turn out a good critical paper, he will worry that if an equal amount of consistent diligent effort had gone into the writing of a poem or a short story, *that* would have been more to the point.

One of the persistent worries of the young writer is that he or she has not lived long enough to have acquired enough experience about which to write. When this problem is raised, I always turn to Flannery O'Connor, who was often asked at her public appearances how a young writer can find enough subject matter for his books. Her answer was usually the same each time the question arose: anyone who has survived childhood has enough information about life to last him the rest of his life.

The complaints are all real and justified. One writes to please a teacher because he is the only reader of the paper. By analyzing a novel one can easily kill it or kill the enjoyment of it. Graduate school means the acquisition of endless meticulous erudition, and a still more dramatic need to please the professors whose recommendations are indispensable for the first job. Where is there a congenial stimulating community where literature is discussed? Does any college, any university provide this?

I try to answer such questions in this way: It is true, Shakespeare never took graduate courses, but James Joyce did, and Samuel Beckett did. If you do go to graduate school and teach afterward, there is no longer an absolute rule saying you will have to become and remain a scholar in the traditional sense. Robert Penn Warren did not. Howard Nemerov did not. And these men continued teaching and writing and publishing. The writing of course papers should not prevent other kinds of writing. When students say they are drained of time and energy for real writing, they are making excuses for laziness.

There is no such thing as a literary community, not even in such a congenial atmosphere as Bennington or Harvard Square or Saint-Germain-des-Prés. The writer is a lonely man. He has to be. It is almost better for him not to talk about his writing, or about the writing of others that is being done today. The so-called literary groups in Greenwich Village or San Francisco or Paris or London are not very inspiring and not very literary.

To be a writer means precisely to avoid such groups and to learn to live deeply within oneself. It means giving up many things of a social order. It means contemplating and understanding one's own life, no matter how limited and monotonous and prosaic it seems to be. It means reading a book, not for pleasure in the usual sense, but for learning more about mankind outside of one's own life and in a language that ennobles the human spirit. It means being grateful for every pain in one's body, for every lack in one's life, for every heartache and every disappointment in love, for every bruise a friend or foe gives one. These are the subjects a writer uses. He is not exactly like other human beings.

PART IV

Three-Quarters of a Century

CHAPTER 9

Poetry Magazine *Is Seventy-Five Years Old (1912–1987)*

In November 1986 I received a letter from Professor William Carter announcing plans for a Proust festivity to be held in Birmingham, at the University of Alabama, in the fall of 1988. It would be the anniversary year, the seventy-fifth, celebrating the first publication of *Du Côté de chez Swann (Swann's Way)* in 1913. Bill Carter invited me to give the last lecture of the symposium, and asked me to use as the title of my talk, "Swann is Seventy-Five Years Old." I accepted this honor and reminded Mr. Carter and his committee, somewhat flippantly, that if I reached the fall of 1988 I would be eighty years old and should perhaps be celebrated myself for being five years older than Swann!

The following month I received a second letter concerned with the age of seventy-five. Joseph Parisi, the editor of *Poetry*, informed me of a project in Chicago to bring out in 1987 a large issue to celebrate the seventy-fifth year of the magazine, which had been founded in 1912 by Harriet Monroe. He asked me to write about my association with the magazine. For twenty years, 1950–70, I served as "foreign editor" under more than one editor; my relationship with *Poetry*, however, antedates 1950 and has continued since 1970.

Long before 1950, during my last two years in high school in Brookline, Massachusetts, I typed out on my first typewriter, a Royal portable, my first poems and sent them to a Chicago address:

232 East Erie Street, for many years the site of *Poetry: A Magazine of Verse* (as it was then called). I had acquired the habit of reading the magazine in the Brookline Public Library and each month automatically checked to see if Harriet Monroe's name was on it, with the founding year of 1912. East Erie, 232, had an element of magic for me, a promise of recognition, a dream to be realized. Every poem I submitted during the next few years, well into my college years, was returned to me, with the familiar rejection slip, without comment. I persevered stubbornly. Today I am grateful no poem of mine written in those years was accepted.

From writing poems I turned to writing criticism, to writing about poems and about poets, and this change of style and genre eventually brought about my relationship with *Poetry*. It was a literary love affair I have always cherished. It initiated friendships with successive editors and work for those editors, each of whom gave me a different title. If I remember correctly, Karl Shapiro appointed me in 1950 as "associate editor." Henry Rago, who succeeded Karl in 1955, called me "foreign editor." Henry knew I was an American but implied in his title that I was also pseudo-French, and gave over to me most of the translations, from a variety of languages, that came to the magazine office. He requested editorial comment on them of acceptance or rejection. From time to time, when Karl or Henry did not agree with the assistant editors over a new manuscript, I would be asked to examine the text and vote yes or no.

I dislike being a judge of anything or anyone. The role I enjoyed the most during my twenty-year appointment was that of "chronicler." At least that is what I called myself when I turned in to Karl or to Henry short critical pieces both on living French poets such as Saint-John Perse, Henri Michaux, René Char, and on a few of the great who, though deceased, I felt should be kept in the minds of the readers of *Poetry*: Baudelaire, Mallarmé, Valéry, Claudel, Max Jacob.

Whenever a sense of guilt overcame me about taking up too much space in the magazine with French poets, Julia Bowe, a fervent sponsor of *Poetry*, would urge me to "keep the articles coming." Whenever I spent an evening with the Bowes, with Julia and Gus, she began to refer to my ever-lengthening list of contributions as a disguised course on French poetry.

Once in 1952 Karl confided an entire issue to my editorial direction. I called it "Post-War French Poets." And once, under Henry's regime, he entrusted me with half an issue (August 1963): "Four French poets." I have always taken pride in my major contribution: the publication of two large parts of Saint-John Perse's poem *Amers* (*Seamarks*). Twice we published in *Poetry*, in French and English, parts of *Seamarks*. Saint-John Perse, who was then living in Washington where he used the name Alexis Léger, was very eager to have these sections of his new work appear in *Poetry*, prior to the publication of the poem as a whole. His letters to me at that time testified to his high esteem for the magazine. I served as mediator between the urgency of the poet in Washington and the difficulty for both Karl and Henry to find sufficient space in the magazine for both the original French of the text and my translation.

How did all of this come about? Chance encounters rule our lives more than we realize. Karl Shapiro resigned his post at Johns Hopkins in 1950 in order to take over the editorship of *Poetry*. The need to change the old address on East Erie, and the need to reduce rental expenses, had become crucial. Stanley Pargellis, the librarian at the Newberry Library, graciously offered space to the magazine and at the same time offered an apartment to Karl and his family in an extensive apartment building owned by the Newberry and very close to it. I had just applied for and received a Newberry Fellowship for three months' work there. As a "fellow" I was also given an apartment which turned out to be close to the Shapiros. We met and became friends, and Karl, eager to find new helpers, immediately appointed me to the staff of editors.

More than that, he asked me to replace him during January 1951 in the course on poetry he was conducting at the University of Iowa. Each of five Mondays I took the train from Chicago to Iowa City to teach the poetry workshop at the university, in the program directed by Paul Engle. I was told by Karl and Paul to teach five sessions on "the art of translation."

For the first Monday I carried with me five sets of manuscripts, poems turned in to Karl by five of the students. I was to read the poems, study Karl's comments on them, and see each of the five students privately and add my own comments, if I had any to add!

I was held especially by the poems of W. D. Snodgrass (a new name for me) and enjoyed talking with him about the personal, intimate mood of the poems and their autobiographical makeup. (At the end of the decade, in 1959, Knopf published Mr. Snodgrass's first book, *Heart's Needle*.)

I often passed by the main office of *Poetry* in the library, not far from my own office. One morning a striking young woman was seated at the desk. I had not seen her before at that spot. When I realized I was staring, apologetically I said, "I feel I have seen you somewhere, seen your face and your red hair, but I can't remember where it was."

Her smile turned more knowing. "Do you come from Boston?"

"I come from the next town."

"Do you know the Gardner Museum?"

That was all I needed. "The big Sargent painting on the top floor."

"She is my ancestress. I am Isabella Gardner."

Even as a youngster I had looked at that portrait of the famous Mrs. Gardner, and now in Chicago I remembered even more than the life-sized portrait the perpetual bunch of fresh violets placed at the foot of the picture.

The cold of that Chicago winter seemed warm to me because of such encounters and so many new friends associated with *Poetry*. Henry Rago, destined soon to replace Karl as editor, introduced me to Julia and Gus Bowe, to Marion Strobel, and then to Haydn Carruth and John Frederick Nims, both to serve eventually as editors. They formed an extraordinary group of poets and readers and lovers of poetry. How privileged I was to belong to such a group during two winters in the fifties and sixties when I worked in the Newberry Library!

Stanley Pargellis was a generous benefactor, a *grand seigneur* who allowed us to poach on his land, although he seemingly had no special interest in the cause of poetry. Marion Strobel was very modest about her poems published in the magazine. In practical ways she was of great help by giving financial guidance and by her efforts to strengthen the precariousness of budgets and bookkeeping.

Karl Shapiro and Henry Rago were admirable editors, poets themselves, intent on maintaining and raising the standards of the magazine. *Poetry* had published carefully edited issues every month since 1912, without intermission in wartime, and had paid contributors for every poem and every page of prose. This record places *Poetry* at the top of all "little" magazines in the country.

Karl was an impassioned man. I knew that from his book *Essay on Rime* (1945), a veritable *ars poetica*, but I knew it also from our conversations on poetic method and on the criticism of poetry. Gradually I became aware of Karl's rejection of Pound and Eliot, and of the major tenets being expounded by the new critics. I imagine he was writing during that winter, when we met very often, his hostile critical stand, *Beyond Criticism* (1953). This attitude saddened me. He denounced too easily what he termed avant-garde pretentiousness, and even symbolism and metaphysics in contemporary poetry. His attack on Marianne Moore caused me the most pain. I tried to forget the attacks and to think of Karl as the best exponent of English prosody I have known. He was an engaging, sympathetic, and helpful friend whom I have missed since my early *Poetry* years.

Without my apprenticeship under Karl, I would not have had such professional courtesy shown me by Henry Rago. Henry and I were good friends at the University of Chicago before he became editor of *Poetry*. We were closer in our philosophical and even theological views on poetry than Karl and I had been. I can remember no moment of controversy or contradiction with Henry. He urged me to continue the articles on the new (and old) French poetry. His friends became mine, especially the Bowes and the Carruths, and John and Bonnie Nims. He was proud of his editorship. His early death was a shock to the small literary world in Chicago of which he was the most animated, the most witty, and the most serious member.

We devised an efficacious way of balancing the budget. Each

year an eminent poet was invited to give a reading of his work. The tickets were moderately priced, but at the end of the evening whichever of the poet's manuscripts and letters had been found in the magazine's files were auctioned, and almost always the receipts were high.

After a few years we came to the most eminent name of all: T. S. Eliot. He accepted to read, tickets were put on sale, and the house was sold out very early. But there was no manuscript from Eliot—his poems and letters to the magazine had been typed. The most famous poem ever published by *Poetry* was "The Love Song of J. Alfred Prufrock." It had appeared in one of Harriet Monroe's early issues. A member of the board approached Mr. Eliot and asked him if he would be willing to copy out the "Love Song" and allow it to be auctioned after his reading. The poet carefully wrote out his long poem. It was sold, thanks to a skillful auctioneer, for $10,000. Our survival for at least one more year was thus assured.

Among the richest memories of my Chicago years and my association with *Poetry* is that of a brilliant critic and professor of English. Morton Dauwen Zabel, after teaching for several years at Loyola University (Chicago), joined the English department at the University of Chicago in 1946, the same year that I joined the university's humanities division. We knew of one another largely because of Yaddo, the center in Saratoga, New York, where Morton was a member of the board and where I was a frequent guest.

He introduced me, quite literally, to the city of Chicago. He guided me through buildings and parks, stores and concert halls. For the final revelation he had reserved a room in the university library: the Harriet Monroe room—a treasure house of books that had come to *Poetry* through the years, books and periodicals related to Harriet Monroe, bound copies of the magazine, letters, manuscripts.

Of all the places he had shown me, Morton was proudest of the small and elegant library room where the literary past of Chicago was enshrined. He introduced me to the librarian and guardian of the collection, Mrs. Bond, the wife of professor Donald Bond, a colleague of Morton's in the English department.

Mrs. Bond listened, as I did, to Morton's eulogy. With the amazing accuracy of details that always characterized his speech, he rehearsed part of his life as he spoke. He had become acquainted with Harriet Monroe in 1926 and began then contributing verse and criticism. She named him associate editor in 1928. During the following years he wrote editorials, reviews, reports on American and European periodicals, and verse of his own for *Poetry*. At Harriet Monroe's death, Morton served as editor for one year—a difficult year of many problems and adjustments.

Poetry represented for Morton Dauwen Zabel a chief glory of his adopted city (he came originally from Minnesota). He revered it with an ardor I never sensed in the other friends and editors of the magazine. That day as we stood in the Harriet Monroe room, it became for me part library, part chapel. And I did not know that day in 1946 that five years later I too would have a modest role as helper and assistant editor.

CHAPTER 10

Swann Is Seventy-Five Years Old
(1913–1988)

I read *Un amour de Swann* at nineteen, just a few years after Proust had died. By twenty I had finished reading *A la recherche du temps perdu* in the old sixteen-volume Gallimard edition. I am still reading it, now in the three-volume Pléiade edition, and still marveling at how much I discover in it at each new reading.

When in November 1986 Professor William Carter assigned me the topic "Swann is Seventy-Five Years Old," I felt at first that such a subject might limit me if I participated in the Birmingham Proust celebration, set for November 1988. Would it prevent me from developing some thoughts concerning Proust's novel that I might wish to discuss? After all, Swann is not all of Proust's novel —neither the character Charles Swann nor that first volume *Du Côté de chez Swann*. As possible thoughts and plots for my lecture began to form in my mind and in my memory, I realized that, indeed, Swann is all of Proust's novel. His presence is in all those aspects of the novel we study and cherish and which we name in turn "psychological, sociological, aesthetic." But uppermost in our remembrance of *A la recherche* is Swann in his human relationships with so many of the characters, especially of course with Marcel. He is friends, often close friends, with many of the Guermantes, with Charlus, with the *duc* and *duchesse,* with the *prince* and *princesse.* Swann knows and admires the three characters who represent accomplishments in creative work: Bergotte, the novelist friend of his daughter; Elstir, the painter whom he knows first as M. Biche in the Verdurin circle; and the composer Vinteuil, whose sonata makes real to him his love for Odette.

Yes, Swann is more pervasive and more present in the novel than any other character, save Marcel in his dual role as narrator and protagonist. The reasons seem to be twofold. There is a great deal of Marcel Proust in Swann, and the character Marcel in the novel seems to derive in part from Swann, who guides the boy and the man in his tastes, his intuitions, his actions, in his capacity for love, and in his very special understanding of love. It would not be too hazardous to propose the thesis that Swann and Marcel in an essential way form one character.

We are introduced to Swann very early in *Swann's Way*, and his appearance is associated in the mind of the young boy Marcel with a sound. The family is on vacation in Combray where they stay in Tante Léonie's house. After dinner they usually spend some time in the garden. The ringing of the garden gate bell announces the arrival of their neighbor, M. Swann, who comes at that time to join them. This event is described as a frequent occurrence. But soon after that opening passage the ringing of that bell is described late one special evening when Swann has been dining with the family and the boy Marcel is in his room upstairs, anguished over not having his usual goodnight kiss from his mother. He hears the bell and knows that it means Swann has left and that soon he may have the chance to have that kiss.

Three thousand pages later in the novel, on the very last page, Marcel, a middle-aged man attending a social reception in the new house of the Guermantes, hears again the sound of that bell: *le tintement de la clochette*. His memory becomes audible after he has met and talked with many of the friends he has known throughout his life. His oldest and greatest friend was Swann, who has died. That evening he had talked with Swann's wife (now Mme de Forcheville), with Swann's daughter (now la marquise de Saint-Loup), and with Swann's granddaughter, Mlle de Saint-Loup.

The sound of the garden gate bell at Combray, so many years later, in the grandest of all the social events in the novel, was the memory of Swann. As a boy, when he heard the bell he knew that

M. Swann was leaving his aunt's house. When he hears it again on the last page of the novel we are tempted to accept it as the signal for Marcel to leave the house of the Guermantes and begin a new life as the author of his book. *Le tintement de la clochette* is not merely an echo Proust speaks of on his last page. It is a gracious recall of Swann, the most gracious of all the Proustian characters. It is one of the most deeply felt sentimental mourning moments in the novel for the reader. And it is also for the reader the ultimate sign of the novel's structure. *Le tintement de la clochette* points to the final words that come just a few words later: *dans le Temps*. Chronological time is uppermost in our usual reading of those last pages of the book. But the sound of the bell Marcel hears is that of triumph over the passing of time. It is the last instance we have of involuntary memory.

The manner of Proust's writing makes it difficult for us to see a unified picture of any of the major characters. We often have the impression that we are seeing just a silhouette of the duchess or a series of fugitive poses of Charlus. Each one is fused with a milieu— Norpois, for example, or Françoise—and each one remains close to the impressions and sentiments of Marcel, whether it be Albertine or Morel. In our hope to see a unified picture of a given character, we forget that Proust was writing a memoir book. Memories are often a series of anecdotes.

And yet Swann is a living character, both before and after his death. At his first appearance in Combray three descriptive details are given which are often repeated later: *nez busqué, yeux verts, cheveux presque roux*. It is little to go on, but perhaps it is enough: the arch of his nose, the green of his eyes, and the ruddiness of his hair. There is only one detail on his closeness to Marcel's family: Swann's father, a stockbroker, was a friend of Marcel's grandfather.

More than one critic has pointed out the three poles or three centers around which Proust constructs his novel: love, society, and art. When we read the second chapter of *Swann's Way: Un amour de Swann*, we realize that single chapter, almost isolated by itself, exemplifies the theory. There Swann appears in his triple function of lover, man of the world, and amateur (or lover of the arts). Proust uses Swann for his first study of passion, the basis of all subsequent studies of passion in *A la recherche*. As we watch Swann in the Verdurin coterie, Proust gives us an image of a Paris world. Swann is a connoisseur—of Italian painting; of architecture, when he describes the church at Balbec to the boy Marcel; and of the Dutch painter Vermeer, about whom he intends to write a study. Swann retains his place among the amateurs of art and does not become a writer.

In the first chapter, *Combray*, Swann is a mysterious figure for Marcel's family. Amiable and courteous, elegantly dressed, Swann is appreciated by them as a friendly neighbor, but they have no understanding of his high social situation. This is the first of many social situations involving erroneous beliefs that Proust treats, very often humorously, throughout the novel. Swann is among the first people outside his family to whom Marcel is attracted and whom he admires. Swann talks to him, gives him copies of Italian paintings, and tells him about Bergotte. Marcel's avidity to learn is nurtured by Swann who leads the boy away from family conversations to those about art and ideas.

The term "psychic pluralism" explains a quality of Proustian characters: the multiple traits in a man's character which often contradict one another, and which surprise and puzzle the reader, as they surprise other characters in the novel. Swann and Charlus are leading examples of psychic pluralism. We know Swann first as the son of a Jewish stockbroker, a member of the Jockey Club, a friend of the Prince of Wales. Yet this friendly neighbor in Combray is considered by Marcel's family a *déclassé*. He has married Odette, a courtesan, as she is called. She is not invited with her husband to the dinner at Combray, and in Paris Marcel's father does not invite Swann to the dinner for Norpois.

After his frenzied and jealous love for Odette comes to an end, Swann marries her, and thus possibly endangers his social life. The marriage does not change his social life greatly. Most of his friends continue to see him, even if some of them ostracize Odette, notably Marcel's family. We continue to think of him throughout the work as a lover, socialite, and art connoisseur, and, because of fidelity to his race, as a defender of Dreyfus. Even that stand did not very much affect his social life; it turned him back to the origins of his race, visible at the end of his life in the modifications of his face. He knew the disease that was to take his life was fatal, and he was resigned, in a very noble way, to death.

Less than a character, Swann is best characterized as a witness, a presence in the book. He is not given the powerful relief that Proust gives to le baron de Charlus in that man's actions and behavior. Swann is a quieter personage, a more finely drawn representative of his historical moment and milieu than Charlus is. Reserved and dignified, yes, but Swann is also a man who throughout the first half of the novel quietly reveals the experiences of his life to Marcel, thus providing the future novelist with the subject matter of his book. I have now come to my sermon text. We are again at the end of the work, on the last page of *Le Temps Retrouvé*, where the name of Swann is evoked more deliberately and explicitly than in any other part of the novel.

The reception scene is in a way a review of all of Marcel's life. He has just received the revelation that will force him to write his book. He is convinced, in an almost abrupt way, that his book is in him. This leads him to a second realization. He says, "The subject matter of my experience, the subject matter of my book, came to me from Swann" (*la matière de mon livre me venait de Swann*).

At the end of the matinée scene of *Le Temps Retrouvé*, which is the end of the novel, Marcel has just seen coming toward him, at Gilberte's side, a girl of sixteen. "Time," he says to himself, "had materialized itself in this girl." Then he names her: "Mlle de Saint-Loup was standing in front of me." He notices that her nose, in the form of a beak and curved, was not like that of Swann but like Saint-Loup's. Marcel ends his description of her by saying that this girl, Swann's granddaughter, was like his own youth.

Then, in a striking analogy, unexpected at this point but allowing Proust once again to reconstruct his novel, he compares the book to a culinary creation of Françoise, that *boeuf à la mode* which M. de Norpois had found so delicious. He then makes a statement crucial for our understanding of Proust's art. "Impressions," he writes, "derived from many girls, from many churches, from many sonatas, will combine to form a single sonata, a single church, a single girl." There we read the origin of the Vinteuil sonata, of Saint Hilaire, and of Albertine.

These thoughts lead Marcel inevitably to the conclusion of the novel, related to that volume of his childhood drama, *le drame de mon coucher*. It is George Sand's *François le Champi*. Before the quieting experience of his mother's reading from that pastoral novel, he had heard the sound of M. Swann's departure. "I had heard the garden gate open, give a peal of its bell and close." *J'avais entendu la porte du jardin s'ouvrir, sonner, se refermer.*

Like a motif on these last pages, the word *mon livre* returns over and over again—the book whose subject matter came to him from Swann. He analyzes this thought meticulously. That is why I called it a sermon text, lending itself to interpretation and study. Marcel reviews his book before writing it. Swann is seen here to be the dominant figure in Marcel's life. Swann's daughter Gilberte was his first love. Swann aroused in him the desire to go to Balbec. If he had not gone to Balbec, he might never have met Albertine and several members of the Guermantes family—Mme. de Villeparisis, Charlus, Robert de Saint-Loup. He might never have met Elstir. It is a passage of gratitude to Swann for his knowledge of Balbec.

He does call this passage about Swann *un pédoncule un peu mince,* a thin or slender stalk, the extent of his life. But he insists that he finally got to know Guermantes Way because he had first known Swann's Way.

Thanks to the sympathy, the advice, and the example of Swann, Marcel, at the end of *Le Temps Retrouvé,* and Marcel Proust, in 1909, began the momentous journey into the past that absorbed all of his energy and all of his genius. He wrote a work of art that was undoubtedly at the same time an act of expiation. This duality may not be exceptional. I tend to believe that many masterpieces in all the arts may have their genesis in a will to expiate. I sense this in the Ninth Symphony, in Fra Angelico's fresco *The Annunciation*, in the Cathedral of Chartres, yes, even in *Ulysses*.

Beauty does more than embellish life. It is a reality (as Proust might say), more important than life. This thought, so pervasive

throughout the work, is often joined with a seemingly contradictory moral theory: namely, that the world is a baffling maze of
illusions. This is apparent in what is for me the most tragic passage
of the novel, when Swann, condemned to death by a specialist,
visits his great friend the *duchesse*. At one moment in their conversation he tells her of his illness. This scene is at the end of *Le côté
de Guermantes*. Oriane refuses to believe Swann and thus spoil her
evening of three social events. More perhaps than merely an example of the Guermantes' egoism and self-centeredness, her refusal
is cruelty, unconscious cruelty, which does infest the universe of *A
la recherche du temps perdu*. It does not poison it wholly. Life survives,
after all. The Proustian characters have an unusual resilience, and
yet almost all of them are at bay, in some form.

This resilience of character is especially visible in Marcel, who
enters the experience of another person. He becomes Swann for
the duration of Swann's love affair with Odette. Proust believed
that our social personality is built up by the ideas of others. Man
is compact of ambiguities. These are the contradictions and con-
trasts in human nature, the heights and depths of human nature.
"Cruelty" would seem to be the Proustian synonym for "pride,"
the gravest of all sins in orthodox belief. Swann has to die before
his good friend the duchesse will receive his daughter Gilberte. By
taking the name of her adoptive father, Forcheville, Gilberte begins
to abolish the memory of her father. It is as Mlle de Forcheville that
she marries a Guermantes, Robert de Saint-Loup.

At the midpoint of the novel, in *Sodome et Gomorrhe*, the evening
party given by the Prince and Princesse de Guermantes, Proust
draws his final portrait of Swann, whom I would call without much
hesitation his favorite hero. We see the prophet's beard, surmounted
by a huge nose. The background of the portrait is Swann's suffering from a mortal illness and from the Dreyfus Affair. His strength
now is his solidarity with his race.

Proust rarely exhibits any preference, but I believe he does here
in this last appearance of Swann, when he seems to be saying to
us that a race does not alter its attributes. In the long episode of

the reception of the Prince and Princesse, we have an outstanding example of Proust's skill at chronicling a social milieu at a given moment in time. It is also filled with passages of introspective self-examination. In its center, with the figure of Swann as he speaks first to the Prince and then to Marcel, we move far into the past of an ancient ancestry, and we move ahead into the future where we faintly foresee a renewed suffering of that race. Swann appears in this passage as an ancient Hebrew prophet. Proust, as the author of the passage, appears as the prophet of the increasingly complex world of modern man. In his novel, Proust moves away from materialism and positivism, and attempts to explain the world in terms of society, history, art . . . God.

I often think of this scene as one of crossroads, important *carrefours,* where the novelist insists on the subconscious recesses of a man's inner life, and at the same time rehearses themes of history and literature. Proust as chronicler and Freud as psychiatrist come close to one another in such episodes.

Like most teachers of Proust, I remind my students, when we are reading the entire work, that the opening pages on *Combray* are never really absent from the rest of the novel. *Combray,* in which Swann plays a reserved quiet role indispensable for all that follows, returns to us like invigorating air of the countryside. There we see peasants, a country doctor, a lady hastening to mass and hoping to get there before the Elevation, shopkeepers, a grocery boy adding to his principal job many others.

This return, this reiteration of *Combray,* may help explain a mysterious statement made at the end of Iris Murdoch's recent novel, her twenty-second novel, *The Good Apprentice* (1985). I have always felt that her art of fiction is close to Proust's. In the passage on the last page of her book, she refers specifically to Proust. It is a reunion scene between a father and his two grown sons. Harry, the father, asks his son Edward, "What's that book you're reading?" "Oh— Proust." Edward had been looking for the passage about Albertine going out in the rain on her bicycle, but he couldn't find it. He had turned to the beginning: *Longtemps je me suis couché de bonne heure.* "What a lot of pain there was in those first pages. What a lot of pain there was all the way through. So how was it that the whole thing could vibrate with such a pure joy? This was something which Edward was determined to find out."

I have never encountered in any other book such a statement about "the pure joy vibrating throughout Proust's book." But I do recognize that undercurrent of joy that rises from the sheer creating of the work. In an interview-article on this recent novel, published in *L'Express*, as she discusses other novelists—Henry James, Dostoyevski, Tolstoy—Murdoch indicates that Proust is her favorite novelist; "*il est mon préféré,*" she said to the Paris interviewer.

If I ever attempted to explain that "joy vibrating throughout the novel," I would turn to Swann—not so much to his character as to his spirit, which is something truer than character. His spirit is both mysterious and constructive. He is powerful with natural wealth, the wealth of nature. The words used by Proust to describe Swann and his actions and charm flow through those pages like a river that brings sweet water to us the readers. His scenes with Marcel, with Odette, with the Prince, with Oriane, with Gilberte, are scenes of crosspollenizing, as if he were the sun in the sky, drawing out what is hidden and causing it to flower as if it were a heliotrope.

In this novel of one million words, the artist is the man who regains time. The famous flashback of *Un amour de Swann* is the first elaborate example. After his marriage with Odette de Crécy, Swann becomes a passionless husband, proud of her beauty, proud that Odette attracts so many men to "her day."

But Swann is not a true artist—no extratemporal recognition comes to him. Long after his death, at the final party, the final matinée, Odette looks much as she ever did. Life had given her some good parts. The Swann-Odette story prefigures the Marcel-Albertine story, in somewhat the same way that the Old Testament prefigures the New Testament, for medieval and Renaissance exegetes.

It would seem that in Proust's mind Marcel and Swann are linked, joined in sensibility, in ambition, and in the place they occupy in the Faubourg Saint-Germain, despite their birth and their early lack of social connections. The temperamental affinities between Swann and Marcel are sketched at the beginning of the novel, and are clearly heard at the end of the novel in the sound of the bell. Proust needed both Marcel and Swann in order to reveal the paradoxical character of our human condition, and thus to humanize the universe. To humanize it and also to discover in it its mystical origins.

A few of the recent critics (I am thinking of Jefferson Humphries), as well as some of the older critics (Fernandez, for example, and Cattaui), find in Proust traces of orphism and the religion of the gnostics—that is, traces of Greek antiquity and the first two centuries of Christianity. It is expressed in a nostalgia for a return to a primitive unity, or in a mourning over the fear that this primitive unity has been lost. Gérard de Nerval, one of Proust's favorite authors, had felt this in his effort to pierce "those gates of ivory and horn that separate us from the invisible world" (*ces portes d'ivoire et de corne qui nous séparent du monde invisible*).

The word "metamorphosis" could serve as a title for the novel in designating the cycle of *Temps perdu* and *Temps retrouvé*. The final appearance of Swann is almost a transfiguration. An impressionist painter like Elstir, so sympathetic to Swann, could not look at a flower without transplanting it in the interior garden of his mind. As Swann listened to *la petite phrase* of Vinteuil's sonata and, much later, as Marcel listened to Vinteuil's septet, each drew an experience, a new understanding of experience, from the silence and the dark that surrounded the compositions. Vinteuil's music reawakened both Swann (in *Un amour de Swann*) and Marcel (in *La Prisonnière*).

Several generations of educated American youth (educated if they took the right courses) have grown up in what I would call a Proustian climate. For the final exam in my Proust course, I list for one question three or four major characters and ask the students to write a portrait of one of those characters and discuss his or her important scenes. If Swann is on the list, and he usually is, eighty to eighty-five percent of the students choose him. They like Swann. They feel secure with him. He is one of the few characters who do not shift their sexual preferences.

The Swann-Odette love affair does not mystify them as it did earlier generations. Swann, for the new readers today, prefigures the anguish of "sickly" love, the lack of will power and jealousy which punctuate every subsequent love story in the novel. I am trying to say—awkwardly, I know—that our manner of falling in and out of love, and complacently undergoing the tortures of jealousy, has become Proustian.

My students today, in reading Proust, understand more lucidly than readers of my generation when we were youthful readers the fact that, like most characters in the novel, Swann leads a double life and is himself ambivalent. He cherishes languid-appearing women, Botticelli-like, in art, and yet in real life he very concretely makes love to servants, to unrefined country girls, to *midinettes,* who resemble Rubens portraits.

In this haunting gallery of characters that Proust gives us (tragic and ludicrous characters), I find that le baron de Charlus is the incomparable figure in this work of fiction. Yet Swann, less dominant, shows Proust's power of character presentation and delineation. Swann is a blend of several persons observed in reality. Marcel as a child senses the mystery that surrounds Swann. He is excited by this mysteriousness, and throughout the story he accumulates contradictions in this friend and counselor. Behind Swann is Proust who unites in himself contradictory qualities. Proust's penetration into a man's emotions and thoughts—I am thinking especially of Swann—is hardly equaled anywhere.

I often ask myself—and also my students on days when they seem eager to contradict me—what gave Proust this power of penetration. I would call it the power of imagination, that goddess "imagination" worshiped by Coleridge, Poe, Baudelaire, and Proust. Imagination—I am thinking again of *Un amour de Swann*—constitutes the whole of love, according to Marcel Proust. If I take this thought one step farther, I would claim that imagination, enriched by a transfiguring memory, transmutes vices and jealousies into beauty, into joy—if I use Iris Murdoch's word.

Every time I read about Swann's love affair with Odette, I am struck by the details of that narrative. As a reader continues with the other parts of the novel, Swann's love for Odette turns almost into a myth or an emblem that loses its realism with the passage of time. Yet it is there, expanded into the other love affairs. They are bigger stories; Swann's love turns into a miniature. In terms of their love, Swann and Odette are mythologized. Swann, like Don Giovanni in Leporello's notebook, is remembered for the number of his love affairs with duchesses and seamstresses. Odette is remembered as *la grande cocotte* that she was, with her many pasts, each one of which provided her with a different name.

We read in the text that Odette was not Swann's type. So he transformed her into Zipporah, a wife of Moses, as painted by Botticelli. This was carried out by the power of imagination and by the accompanying power of illusion. Swann talks not so much about the character of Odette, as about her love of flowers, of orchids and chrysanthemums. Marcel, in his love for Odette, continues to relate her to flowers. He sees her first across the hawthorn hedge lining Tansonville. Later, going even farther than Swann in his comparison of Odette with flowers, Marcel sees the Bois de Boulogne, with its flowers and flowering trees, as the Elysian Garden of woman, because Mme Swann once walked there.

The hawthorns and the lilacs of *Swann's Way* form one part of what I think we can call the Dantesque voyage of the narrator through his childhood and his loves, his *Vita Nuova*. The emblematic flowers are as important in the formative years of Marcel as the spires of Martinville and the carved medieval stones of Saint-André-des-Champs. Recently in a museum, on examining several paintings of Marc Chagall, I was struck by the theme of childhood they draw upon. Bridal couples, fiddlers, and scrolls of the Torah were the milieu of childhood from which the painter had never escaped. I thought then of childhood, so important in *Swann's Way*.

Marcel's childhood was undisturbed by wars and revolutions. It was a time of great events, of great figures close at hand (great actresses) in a world still radiant and mysterious, yet so real that when he reads Genesis the boy can embrace the angels of Abraham. This thought of childhood in the paintings of Chagall and in the text of Proust reminded me that they bear witness to greater knowledge than Proust and Chagall possessed, unconscious knowledge, patriarchal knowledge.

Archetypal symbols of Chagall—the moon, the bride, the angel

—and the archetypal symbols of Proust—the madeleine cakes of
Léonie, the cattleyas of Odette, the stone faces of Saint André—
caused me to reflect that the feminine dominates Chagall's paintings
and *A la recherche*. The understanding strength of the grandmother,
and the life story of Mme de Villeparisis, control and delight the
attentiveness of Marcel as much as any male figure in the story,
even Swann.

When in one painting of Chagall a woman under the moon is
seen milking a blue cow, an entire world is revealed. The male and
the female in Proust are contrasted in the scene when Odette is
quiet in her apartment and Swann is outside on the street mistaking
everything in an access of jealousy. The Sabbath candles glow in
Chagall, as the red dress of Oriane glows before the admiring eyes
of Swann.

In the chapter of *Combray* in which Marcel tries to tell us how
important the two ways are for him, Swann's and Guermantes's,
he describes them as a fragment of landscape (*morceau de paysage*)
that floats uncertainly in his mind like a flowering Delos (the Greek
island which once floated before Zeus attached it). A few pages before this passage on flowering Delos, Marcel watches a water lily,
helpless in the current of the Vivonne, and he thinks not only of
Léonie, unable to move from her bed, but also of the spirits in
Dante's hell, unable to leave the circle to which they have been assigned. The passage ends with a reference to Virgil, Dante's guide
who urges him on to the next circle.

During these last few years when I have been teaching a series of
three courses—Dante, the French symbolists, and Proust (in that
order)—I see more and more clearly the relationship between these
works, the dependence of one on the other. My students study
first the role of Virgil as a guide to Dante; then, when they read
Proust it is not hard for them to consider Swann as Marcel's guide
comparable to Virgil in the *Commedia*.

Swann leads Marcel to woman: to Odette first, and then to Gilberte, and then indirectly to Albertine. Swann is guide but also
father, as the dominant figure in Marcel's life. His real father is
hardly heard of again after two early episodes: the goodnight kiss
and the dinner for Norpois.

I have come to look upon the goodnight kiss episode as the cornerstone of the entire novel. As a dinner guest that night, Swann at first deprives Marcel of his mother's kiss. But then a reversal takes place, and because of Swann Marcel is more indulged in than ever when his mother spends that night in his room. We might conclude therefore that Swann leads Marcel to his mother, representing all women, as Virgil leads Dante to Beatrice in the *Divine Comedy*.

CHAPTER 11

Remembering Léonie Adams

The setting is one of the faculty houses on the campus of Bennington College in Vermont. The time is the end of the school year, June 1936, and the end of the last literature faculty meeting. We were trying to turn it into a mildly festive gathering. The business matters had been put aside (academic business matters are never terminated). But we were tired from the end-of-term papers, last conferences with counselees, and from the idea of the commencement weekend rites, to begin the following day.

The critic William Troy and his wife, the poet Léonie Adams, had joined the Bennington faculty in 1935. They had come to us from Washington Square College of New York University, and had weathered very well their first year at the college. Those of us who had been teaching literature for a few years at Bennington were proud they were with us. We had grown to admire them as teachers and new friends. We knew, better than other members of the faculty, better than the students, their literary achievements and what those achievements promised for the future. I sat facing them, Bill and Léonie, and sensed the fatigue in the other three teachers: Kenneth Burke, the oldest and the most eminent, Stanley Edgar Hyman, one of Kenneth's foremost admirers, and, the youngest of us all, the poet Ben Belitt, who several times through the year had spoken to me passionately about Léonie's poems.

There had been a brief silence in the room, as we put papers away.

Then Bill turned to Léonie, as he joked a bit about our obvious despondency. He seldom asked Léonie to do anything in a public way, but the meeting was not really public: we were a close-knit, harmonious faculty group.

"Why don't you read," he said to her, "what you did last month when we called on my sister at her convent. Sister Camilla was delighted with it. It might help perk us up."

We were surprised to learn that Bill had a sister who was a nun, and wondered what Léonie had read to her. We of course seconded Bill's suggestion. She hesitated just a minute or two, and then nodded her head. She was going to read something. We quieted down and waited in great expectancy.

Léonie raised her head, and, without looking at any one of us, spoke in a strong voice she had never used in my hearing. There was no book on her lap or in her hand. She began reciting in that clear loving voice of hers:

> Yet once more, O ye Laurels, and once more,
> Ye Myrtles brown, with Ivy never sear . . .

Ah! It was *Lycidas*. We recognized those lines from Milton. She continued to recite with varied intonations the entire pastoral. We were able to follow it so easily: the shepherd speaking his Doric lay in ancient Greece, and the implied reference to Edward King and his death by drowning in the Irish Sea. From Greece we moved to that other age when Léonie emphasized "the pilot of the Galilean lake."

The spell we were under was not broken until she spoke the last line: "Tomorrow to fresh woods and pastures new." She recited all hundred and ninety-three lines of *Lycidas* quietly, movingly, as if she were celebrating the event of death and the life of nature that was its setting. Her voice changed as she moved from the Aegean to the Sea of Galilee. Milton's memory had become hers during those minutes when the words of the poet held us as steadfastly as the voice of the reader.

And now, fifty years later, and just a few days after Léonie's passing—on June 27, 1988—I am remembering the spell she cast over us that long-ago June day on a Vermont hillside. She caused our weariness to turn into attentiveness. Through the words of the poet, and through Léonie's devotion to poetry, she raised us to a new understanding of why we were there in that particular place, at that particular time.

Certainly, throughout the year, we had felt something of that spiritual power in Léonie. Her spirit had always seemed to us unaffected by trivia, unaffected by the worries that all of us felt as we taught in a school of such rigorous doctrine, where every utterance we made was examined and judged. Léonie was above pedagogical doctrine. She had no need of it. The purity of her spirit was the doctrine she followed. The students had begun to feel this, and we her colleagues and friends basked in that early recognition of the students.

We amused her, teachers and students alike, in our puzzled nervousness. I had watched her as she looked at Bill when, in our faculty meetings, he would rant against a stupid rule. He intended to uproot it, and yet he knew that all the obscure forces of the institution were against him. Somehow Léonie knew that teaching was quite simply communication between two human beings. For its consummation, each one, teacher and student, had to sharpen his mind and his heart so that there would be communication on the highest possible level.

Léonie made no effort in her speech to argue or discuss, because in her thoughts the matter had been solved, and she looked forward to quieting down the irascibility of her husband and his male colleagues. How we needed that feminine spirit! How it helped deflate our momentary scenes of wrath!

She presided over our tempers and silliness, as she presided over the vegetables in her small garden as they sprouted and grew to that moment of perfection when she could take them into her kitchen and prepare them skillfully for Bill—and for Ben and me if we had the good luck to be invited to dinner. Ben's great admiration for Léonie helped me to measure mine. Ben and I were the bachelors on the faculty. We matched one another in our devotion to Léonie, and talked with fervor about small details in her speech and behavior. Quite seriously one evening, after leaving the Troys' apartment, we spoke of the magical way she had cooked a red cabbage!

Ben was familiar with the vegetable, but I was not. It was a gas-
tronomical novelty to me as I savored the taste and asked Léonie
how she had cooked it. The question must have seemed ludicrous
to her. She had boiled it in a big pot, and then cut it up and served
it with butter and a few herbs. She looked at me quizzically with a
smile that said, "Are you serious?" She did add, however, "Bill likes
red cabbage." Every meal was primarily for him. I was convinced
that he was the most spoiled male in Vermont.

As we enjoyed the cabbage, the rice, and the small pieces of lamb,
literary talk started up. Bill and Ben usually disagreed in their opinions about a new book that Bill had just reviewed in *The Nation*. I
would insert a few remarks to keep the quarrel going. Léonie listened and seemed to be forever hoping something significant would
be said. If any slight error was made, in fact or quotation, she would
then intervene, almost under her breath, and thereby prove that she
had looked at the book in question, and had read Bill's review very
carefully.

Long after William Troy's last illness and death in 1961, Stanley
Edgar Hyman edited and published his *Selected Essays* (Rutgers
University Press). Léonie had preserved all of Bill's writings: the
seventy-odd articles and reviews he had published during his life-
time, many of great distinction, and a few unpublished pieces.
Léonie knew their worth, and she cherished Bill's critical method,
so apparent in his articles in *The Nation* during the 1930s, and in the
literary quarterlies in the 1930s and 1940s. As Hyman says, Bill's
"mad Irish perfectionism" kept him from publishing a book of his
writings.

The poet's art of Léonie and the critic's art of Bill were two
different worlds of literature. One of their most noble traits was
the respect and the admiration that each felt for the other's work.
Literary quarrels, in the oral tradition, abounded between Bill and
Léonie when their friends visited with them, but each faithfully
and sincerely praised the literary achievement of the other.

One evening at Bennington, Bill, who often spoke in a somewhat pontifical manner, made a statement as if it were orthodox
doctrine: "We recognize great poetry by its genuineness, by its con-
creteness, and by its definiteness." Léonie had moved to the edge
of her chair as she had listened. She had certainly not expected to

be brought into this very sound but histrionically expressed belief of her husband. Bill, at that moment, turned to her—this was unusual because in public he often seemed to ignore her—and said: "Léonie, your poems have those qualities." It was an ecclesiastical nod of approval. (I had once told Bill that if he had been born one hundred years earlier, he would have become a cardinal in the Church. He laughed, but he was pleased.)

Whatever Léonie touched had the shape of perfection. It might be one of her poems or the carefully aligned vegetables in her garden or the manner in which she read Milton or Hopkins. We could only imagine the quiet, reserved skill of her teaching. Bill was looked upon as a man favored by these examples of perfection joined to his life: poetic, gastronomic, pedagogic, horticultural. All of these achievements were performances, in a way, carried out inconspicuously, effortlessly. Bill's role at Bennington was that of a very impressive teacher. He was eloquent and inspiring when he was teaching one of his favorite books: *Ulysses* or *Le rouge et le noir* or *Madame Bovary*. When in conversation he had lapses of memory or made slight mistakes, Léonie, never too passive, never too overawed in his presence, would correct him in just a few words, specific words that startled him and momentarily irritated him. Only Léonie dared to do this. Certainly no student, no colleague would attempt to put Bill Troy down.

During one of their years at Bennington, the Troys occupied an apartment in the "Hall House" in Old Bennington. The First Church, white and stark, opposite the Hall House, had been restored inside and out. Robert Frost and the members of his family are buried in the cemetery behind the church. The tombstones forming the first line behind the white fence of First Church, lining Monument Avenue, are the oldest. I had often noticed and read to myself the epitaph, carved in stone, that marks the grave of the first pastor:

In memory of the Revd. M. Jedidiah Dewey
First Pastor of the Church in Bennington. . . .

After the date of his death, *Decmbr 21st. 1778,* there were six lines of poetry:

Of comfort no man speak!
Let's talk of graves, of worms,
And epitaphs, make dust our
Paper, and with rainy eyes,
Write sorrow on the bosom
Of the earth.

I had admired the beauty of those lines. One day at lunch in the
college commons I mentioned them to Bill Troy, and asked if he
didn't agree that they sounded like the best eighteenth-century English verse. He replied that he too had been impressed with the
poetry on Jedidiah's tomb, and when once he praised the lines to
Léonie, she quietly answered, "They should be good. They're from
Richard II."

I had often wished I might listen to Léonie teach poetry, but
never asked her if I might attend the lessons. As far as I know, no
one else made such a request either. But on one occasion, in the
Troys' apartment in Old Bennington, I had the good luck to discuss
with Léonie and Louise Bogan a difficult poem of Mallarmé. In
the literary world at that time, especially in New York, the names
of Louise Bogan and Léonie Adams were often joined. They were
friends, and their work had been recognized at about the same time
by the practicing poets.

The college had invited Louise Bogan to give a reading of her
poems. It was a successful performance, and Léonie was gratified.
The following evening I was invited to dine with the Troys, who
were entertaining the visiting poet. Bill retired early, immediately
after dinner. He was suffering from a form of indigestion that often
plagued him. I stayed on with the two ladies. When Miss Bogan
asked me which French poets I was teaching, I told her of my
struggles over Mallarmé with a small group of senior girls. She
was immediately interested, and I seized the opportunity to tell her
about my efforts that afternoon as I prepared a class on the sonnet
"M'introduire dans ton histoire." "No title for that poem," I said.
"You have to make some sense out of the first line." At that remark
Léonie and Louise smiled at one another and reported that once in
New York they had worked together specifically on that sonnet,
intrigued, as I suppose everyone is, by the mysterious first line.

Then, without any copy of Mallarmé at hand, they rehearsed the sonnet line by line, resurrected it integrally, and, before making any strict interpretation, simply enjoyed the beauty of the lines, delighted with their faithful memory. They brought everything more clearly into focus than I had been able to. They loved the mythic reminiscence of the timid hero touching with his bare heel a plot of grass. I had that afternoon sensed the allusion to Achilles, vulnerable only in his heel. Then Léonie pointed out that the moment of conquest for the Mallarmé hero will be a mortal wound or a dying. The line they remembered best was the sun-chariot mounting in the sky, and then sinking down into a ruddy glow. They called the "thunder and rubies" (*Tonnerre et rubis aux moyeux*) the sacramental flashes of combat. We did not know at that time that T. S. Eliot, in his first quartet, *Burnt Norton*, was going to adapt that Mallarmé line into:

Garlic and sapphires in the mud
Clot the bedded axle-tree.

I felt goaded on by my excitement in hearing Léonie and Louise analyze the lines of Mallarmé, and I asked them at the end how they would summarize the sonnet for a class attempting a first reading. Léonie spoke directly to my question when she said: "Mallarmé avoids any direct narration, any specific allusion to the original experience, whatever that was. But the sonnet is the celebration of an experience. It is really the sonnet of a hero and not of a lover."

Walking home that evening through the dark of the Bennington night, I was jubilant with thoughts that I had been enlightened about the sonnet. In the afternoon I had thought of the sonnet as celebrating a sexual conquest. But now it was also for me the course of the sun: a flaming sunset sinking into its own death.

Only once did Léonie talk with me about Paris. I knew that she had spent a year there on a Guggenheim Fellowship, but I had not found the right moment to ask her about her Paris experiences. Not until one evening . . . I was to have dinner with Bill and Léonie. Bill was late in getting home from some counselees in his "barn" office at the college, and Léonie asked me if I would like to have a drink before dinner. "If you have any vermouth, that would be just right—with some ice," I said.

When she handed the glass to me, she smiled and said, "Vermouth always brings back to me my year in Paris."

This was my chance and I asked: "Which was your Guggenheim year?"

"It was 1928." I did not want to interrupt her by saying that my first visit to Paris was the summer of 1928. But I did ask if she was there during the summer.

"Yes, I did almost no traveling that year. I enjoyed living in Paris, although I was very lonely there. Every afternoon, late in the day, I went to the one café I used, the Dôme in Montparnasse. I had a corner table that always seemed empty, and ordered the same drink day after day, from the same waiter. He was a friendly fellow who grew accustomed to my being there at the same time each day. He saved the table for me. I don't drink and had been told that vermouth was the mildest of drinks. So I ordered it each day. It seemed more sophisticated to me than a *citron pressé* or a cup of tea. The waiter and I always exchanged a few words. He was the only person with whom I spoke French. After two months of sitting at the Dôme and watching the people go by on the wide sidewalk, the waiter one day, when there were very few people seated at the café, said to me as he put the glass on my table, 'Madame, do you order vermouth because you believe it to be a harmless drink?'

" 'Yes, that is exactly why I take it.'

" 'But, Madame, it is far from being harmless. It is addictive. If you continue much longer ordering a glass of vermouth every day, you will become an addict. Vermouth is from the absinthe plant. It is the substitute for absinthe because that drink is by law now forbidden in France.' "

Léonie's beautiful small hands had the sprightliness, the liveliness of a lizard in the ruins of a wall. Whatever she observed was seen from an unusual angle, and under a strong light that would throw it into relief. That angle and that lighting protected her poems from any torrential lyricism, as they protected her daily speech.

My generation paid her too little attention. But beginning with the generation of her students at Bennington and at Columbia, and continuing with today's young students of poetry, her genius was discovered and will be rediscovered. During those Vermont years when I lived close to her—at times just a field separating us, at other times three or four miles of road—I was unaware of how much my observations of her meant, how much I learned from our encounters, even very brief ones. She never wandered about, as some of us did, in those woods and back roads. She never grew tired, she never rested. There was no sign ever of disorder in her thinking or in her words.

In my own mind I used to call her "la princesse de Clèves." At that time I was studying the novel of Mme de La Fayette and was delighted to find traits of the princess in Léonie: her reserve, for example, simple but never extreme. I often wondered what she thought of her courtiers—for we were that—eager to have some brief thought spoken from her heart. She loved the spring, and, in memory of the French novel, I would convert the Vermont spring into the richer spring of Touraine. I converted our simple houses into marble staircases, and our faculty meetings into palace intrigues and tournaments. All of these vagaries I kept to myself. It was necessary to tame them as I felt I was moving closer to some understanding of a poet's spirit. . . . So many years pass before we learn how to accept the privileges of our life.

Index

à Wallace Fowlie
avec l'amitié
de
Jean Cocteau
*
1956

Collection of W.F.

Wallace Fowlie is the author of many books: scholarly studies on Proust, Rimbaud, Mallarmé, Gide, Claudel, Stendhal, and Dante, as well as *The Letters of Henry Miller and Wallace Fowlie*, *Characters from Proust* (poems), and *Journal of Rehearsals: A Memoir* (Duke University Press), for which he received the first Harold D. Vursell Memorial Award, given annually by the American Academy and Institute of Arts and Letters "to single out recent writing in book form that merits recognition for the quality of its prose style." Subsequent volumes in his series of memoirs published by Duke University Press are *Aubade: A Teacher's Notebook*, and *Sites: A Third Memoir*.

Wallace Fowlie is James B. Duke Professor Emeritus of French Literature, Duke University.